Issues in International Trade and Development Policy

Issues in International Trade and Development Policy

THEODORE R. MALLOCH

PRAEGER

New York
Westport, Connecticut
London

Library of Congress Cataloging-in-Publication Data

Malloch, Theodore R.
  Issues in international trade and development policy.

  Bibliography: p.
  Includes index.
  1. Commercial policy. 2. Commerce. 3. Economic
development. 4. Economic history—1971–
I. Title.
HF1411.M3325 1987   382'.3   87-11697
ISBN 0-275-92356-8 (alk. paper)

Copyright © 1987 by Praeger Publishers

Library of Congress Catalog Card Number 87-11697
ISBN: 0-275-92356-8

First published in 1987

Praeger Publishers, One Madison Avenue, New York, NY 10010
A division of Greenwood Press, Inc.

Printed in the United States of America

The paper used in this book complies with the Permanent
Paper Standard issued by the National Information Standards
Organization (Z39.48–1984).

10 9 8 7 6 5 4 3 2 1

Contents

Preface

To say that the current atmosphere in the global economy is contentious is to make something of an understatement. The 1980s have been full of disputes between industrialized countries and newly industrializing ones; between developing countries and northern markets over issues of access; and between Japan, the United States, and the European Community (EC) on a whole range of disputes. Some of the most disputatious issues revolve around trade; others linger on in the seemingly forgotten domain of economic development. The two are not unrelated.

Over the past decade international trade has become considerably more important to the U.S. economy. Exports of goods and services have gone from 7 percent of GNP in 1970 to over 13 percent in 1986. Imports now account for over 15 percent of the U.S. market, up from just 6 percent 20 years ago. Economic policies in the United States, including those that deal with development issues in various Third World economies, have a great effect on foreign countries and vice versa. The recovery of the U.S. economy, for instance, has led to an increase of exports from its major trading partners, thus stimulating other economies around the world, as close as Canada and as far off as Timbuktu and Iloilo.

In view of the increased importance of international transactions to the U.S. economy and the close links between the U.S. and foreign economies, it is not surprising that the president and Congress have had much to say about the international economy. In 1985 some three hundred different trade bills were before the Congress. On nearly a weekly basis (it seemed) the president was deciding whether to restrict some imported commodity or merchandise, lower the value of the dollar, recommit himself to voluntary restraints, allow free trade, or deal with the ominous Third World debt.

The broadest measure of U.S. foreign trade, the current account, which measures trade in merchandise and services, posted a record deficit of $101 billion in 1984 and deteriorated further throughout 1985 and on into 1986. The United States also became a debtor nation for the first time since 1914. U.S. industry witnessed devastating imports as a result of the gain in the value of the dollar. These imports occurred across the entire industrial spectrum, not in just one or two insignificant sectors.

With protectionist cries on the rise, U.S. exporters complained loudly about the handicaps imposed by the too-strong dollar, slower growth abroad, and foreign import barriers. Some have questioned long-term U.S. industrial competitiveness, while others hope the pressure of record trade deficits will spawn a new toughness among business leaders. The growing frustration over what to do about trade has also stirred up a great many fears. Fortunately, it has also led to a significant number of new negotiations that will open trade channels wider. Developing, as well as developed countries, stand to benefit from the expansion of world trade. No other area is as important to the economic growth of the less developed countries (LDCs) as trade. Trade promotes the flow of goods, services, and ideas. The ninefold growth in the volume of international trade since World War II reflects the success of the world's trading system. While there are many disputes prevailing in the present atmosphere, few challenge the importance of world trade for economic development.

This volume briefly reviews some significant trends in trade and development policy in the 1980s, then presents ten essays on disputatious trade and development issues. Through looking at different sectors and trade negotiations, the reader will become familiar with a number of areas where trade policy has been sharply debated. Trade-related problems surrounding South-South relations, the prospects for foreign direct investment, and regulation of the pharmaceutical industry are discussed in the context of the North-South dialogue. Understanding the nature of the disputes and the contours of the debates can assist all countries to strive for economic development through global trade.

Issues in International Trade and Development Policy

1

Overview of Trends in the 1980s

The United States registered a record $123.3 billion merchandise trade deficit in 1984, nearly double the $69.3 billion 1983 deficit. The 1985 deficit came close to $150 billion; the 1986 deficit grew even larger.

What has been happening in the 1980s to the U.S. place in the international economy? Most of the growth in the merchandise trade deficit during this decade can be attributed to manufacturers, which account for 92 percent of the trade deficit growth. The deterioration of U.S. performance occurred across most types of products, even high technology goods. Imports of petroleum remain the largest single deficit commodity group in U.S. trade, over $50 billion in 1984, despite a decade of conservation and fuel efficiency.

During the 1980s the United States actually ran trade deficits with most of its major trading partners. Most bilateral trade balances deteriorated further in 1984 and again in 1985. Particularly large deficit increases occurred in trade with Japan ($15.2 billion), the European Community (EC) ($11.8 billion), and the East Asian Newly Industrialized Countries (NICs) ($8.6 billion).

U.S. exports have had a shaky time in the 1980s. Reversing a decline in 1984, performance was still almost 7 percent below the 1981 peak level of $234 billion. Machinery and transport equipment accounted for almost half the growth in exports.

Exports of aircraft, refined petroleum products, and animal feeds posted large decreases. The high dollar was one cause for the deteriorating export picture. Imports, on the other hand, surged year after year. In 1984 they grew by another 26.4 percent to $341.2 billion, with manufacturers accounting for most of the rise. Major increases were witnessed in basic industry inputs, including iron and steel, aluminum, organic chemicals, as well as in capital goods and a wide range of consumer goods.

U.S. trading partners have remained somewhat stable over the 1980s. Sixty percent of total U.S. merchandise trade was with the developed countries. Developing countries accounted for over a third of total trade in merchandise and the centrally planned economies (CPEs) less than 3 percent.

Because of the trade deficit, calls for trade protectionism reached peak levels by 1985. Retaliation against Japan's allegedly unfair trade practices emerged in the Congress as a lead agenda item. But even in the face of all the proposed protectionist legislation, the United States remained the world's leading exporter. The U.S. share of world exports has been about 12 percent since the late 1970s. The so-called deindustrialization of America may be more myth than fact. But the U.S. trade deficit (put into perspective) currently exceeds the gross national product of Saudi Arabia or Sweden. No one believes this is a sign of a robust economy.

Economists have tended to attribute from 50 percent to 75 percent of the current trade deficit to an over-valued dollar. But there are other causes to recall. The economic policies of our industrial trading partners have been less progrowth in the aftermath of the last recession. Some, particularly in Europe, did not adjust to changed global patterns of production and competition. Too often this has meant restraints on access for imports and export promotion, often with heavy subsidies. Debt problems in many developing countries, especially in Latin America, led to the adoption of import barriers and the dumping of exports onto foreign markets. Generating a trade surplus to repay obligations was no easy task for LDCs. One result is that most of these countries bought fewer U.S. goods.

World trade following moderate recovery after three years of stagnation saw slow volume growth in 1985 and 1986. Trade will return to the higher rates of the bygone era only as the world economic recovery spreads and strengthens and as tariff and nontariff barriers are relaxed. If the world's actual real growth rate in the years ahead falls below 2.5 percent, real trade growth will be nearer to zero and international trade activity may not be able to stop protectionism or allay the international debt crisis. As many Organization for Economic Cooperation and Development (OECD) countries continue their tight money policies in response to budget deficits and inflation, there is the possibility that expanding protectionism will dwarf the positive effects of earlier trade rounds and that unilateral trade policy measures will bring about a reaction on a broader, more intensifying set of international trade issues.

ON DEVELOPMENT

During the last three decades the United States has become increasingly intertwined with the LDCs. The economies of many developing countries, especially the Newly Industrialized countries (NICs), have grown to have a significant impact on world trade and finance. Sustained noninflationary growth and open markets in the United States are among the prime reasons for economic growth in LDCs, since the United States is the premier trading nation and the major source of investment funds for developing countries. In the last year U.S. foreign direct investment in LDCs totaled over $50 billion—22 percent of our total private direct investment abroad. U.S. economic assistance to LDCs exceeds that of any OECD country, although our proportion of the total has dropped. The United States also continues to participate in several international commodity agreements, covering such items as natural rubber and coffee. Through multilateral agencies and bilateral programs the United States has served economic, humanitarian, and strategic interests while assisting needy persons and delaying disasters across the Third World.

Trade with the LDCs is increasingly important to the United States accounting for over 30 percent of U.S. exports. The United States exported $75 billion to LDCs while importing $110 billion in 1984. This increased trade is one key to the economic growth of developing countries. For most LDCs, by the mid–1980s trade, not official aid, was the main source of foreign exchange.

The decades of development were successful but much work

remains to be done in the developing countries. Per capita income has risen but will go up further only modestly if current forecasts come true. The major issues in development discussions during the 1980s for repairing Third World economic growth have been (1) reviewing the development policies of the donor countries and international agencies; (2) reviving international capital flows; (3) liberalizing world trade; and (4) improving the economic policies in individual developing countries. The new international development focus is on national performance, both macroeconomic and structural. Even the character of the major international financial institutions in the 1980s, and their functions, appear to reflect an intensified concern with improved policies, privatization, and a more effective use of resources. The 1980s have been depressed times for commodity prices, severe recession, and dropping official development assistance.

I

Trade Problems

2

Renegotiating the Multi-Fiber Arrangement: North Versus South Again

The latest renegotiation of the Multi-Fiber Arrangement (MFA), which expired in July 1986, once again pitted the interests of the less developed countries (LDCs) against those of the developed nations.[1] The talks, which began in Geneva in mid–1986, proved to be the most contentious yet. The initial negotiating positions were (1) liberalization with a gradual return to General Agreement in Tariffs and Trade (GATT) rules (favored in particular by the most competitive LDCs) and (2) substantial retention of the current system (favored generally by developed countries).

A return to GATT rules would imply lower future price increases, expanded output and export earnings in the LDCs and greater adjustment pressures in the developed countries. Liberalization could also create tension among the LDCs as they are forced to compete for markets in developed countries. Retention of the MFA would bring about higher prices for most clothing and some textile products as well as some loss of world economic growth. Quantitative controls on trade would proliferate, limiting export potential of LDCs, particularly for the poorer emerging suppliers.

The negotiating environment appeared more receptive to renewal than to substantial liberalization. The European Community (EC) stood for renewal; the LDCs called for liberalization masking their tenuous unity. The renegotiation included several

An earlier version of this paper was co-authored with William Ross and presented at the American Economic Association Meeting in 1986.

substantive reforms designed to satisfy specific concerns of individual countries. Recent textile trends indicate that

total textile and clothing imports of the seven summit countries[2] have
increased by slightly more than 6 percent per year, just above the
minimum quota growth rate established by the MFA;

the United States provided a far larger import market than the other six
summit countries; and

imports of textiles and clothing produced by the LDCs play a larger role
in the markets of the United Kingdom, the Federal Republic of Germany, and Canada than in the United States, but imported clothing
from major LDCs has been taking 10 percent or more of the U.S. market
since 1979.

The MFA was negotiated in 1973 and entered into force for
four years starting in 1974. It was intended to be temporary, but
it was renewed for a second four years in 1977 (MFA II) and again
in 1982 (MFA III).

Since the early 1950s when the U.S. textile industry experienced severe competition from Japan, it has sought broad protection from imports. Voluntary export controls took effect in
1955; attempts at multilateral action through GATT commenced
in 1959. Under the Short-Term Arrangement (STA) which covered October 1961 to September 1962, textile-exporting countries
accepted restraint in exchange for an assured increase in market
access in the developed countries. The Long-Term Arrangement
(LTA) was in effect from February 1962 until the first MFA.

The protocol of the original MFA (reaffirmed in MFAs II and
III) states four basic objectives:

1. Provision for orderly and equitable development of trade.
2. Prevention of market disruption caused by low-priced imports.
3. Allowance for access to markets for developing countries.
4. Allowance for safeguard action in the form of quantitative restrictions on imports.

The MFA is therefore a global framework for controlled expansion of trade that authorizes bilateral quota agreements between suppliers and importers covering every product believed

to disrupt or to threaten disruption in importers' industries. Under all three MFAs, developed countries agreed in principle to a minimum 6 percent annual import growth rate subject to exceptions. Subsequent bilateral talks arranged consultations on disputed products and provided for cross-category and cross-year quota flexibility.

Textiles and clothing are the only manufactured products exempted from regular GATT rules. (The MFA's non-GATT provisions include discriminatory bilateral treatment and quantitative restrictions). Participating nations retain all other GATT rights and obligations.

The Textile Surveillance Body (TSB) and GATT is charged with supervising the functioning of the arrangement and mediating bilateral disputes. The United States, the EC, and Japan are permanent members of the TSB. Additional members are chosen for annual terms by the other MFA participants. The TSB also reviews all restrictions and agreements negotiated by member countries.

Bilateral agreements on import quantities regulate the system of trade for textiles and apparel. Under the present MFA, the EC has 25 bilateral agreements with developing countries, a unilateral quota on Taiwan, and an informal agreement with China. The United States has 34 bilateral restraint agreements with 29 countries and 9 agreements with non-MFA signatories. Most other industrial importing countries also have bilateral arrangements with LDCs.

LDCs' TEXTILE AND CLOTHING INDUSTRIES

LDCs believe that textile and apparel manufacturing is a "take-off" industry because of its labor-intensive character. The textile and clothing sectors in most Third World countries have grown dramatically over the last few decades. By 1982, textiles and clothing employment exceeded 20 percent of manufacturing employment in 15 countries, 6 of which had figures exceeding one-third. Five countries reported employment in excess of 20 percent for clothing alone.

Textiles and clothing account for one-third of total LDC manufacturing exports and, in some newly industrialized countries, more than 50 percent. In 1963, LDCs provided 21 percent of developed-country textile and clothing imports. By 1982, the figure had reached 55 percent.

In addition to competitive advantage owing to low labor costs, LDC textile and clothing exports have been aided by several types of technological change. These include advances in transportation relating to air freight and containerization and evolution of such improvements in synthetic fibers process as rotor spinning, modernized looms, and computerized production. At the same time, positive economic adjustment in the developed countries has in recent years made them more competitive in some textile categories, particularly those involving capital-intensive production methods.

LDCs AND THE MFA

Many LDCs charge that the MFA has delayed necessary structural adjustment of the world textile and apparel industry. They argue that a growing array of bilateral and unilateral quantitative restrictions on specific products has made the MFA increasingly cumbersome and restrictive. They state that their clothing and textile exports have grown much slower than those of non-MFA participants.

LDCs see rising protectionism in such recent U.S. actions as more frequent calls for consultations on specific import categories, countervailing duty suits against a large number of developing countries, and changes in rule-of-origin regulations. The LDCs view the U.S. market as the largest and most open in the world, and they view any U.S. move that restricts imports as harmful to their industrial expansion, employment growth, and export earnings.

The LDCs also view European nations as increasingly protectionist. LDC exports have been hurt by a complex EC quota system and slow growth of European textile and apparel demand. Developing country exporters are especially concerned by occasional proposals from EC members to lower quota levels and to limit growth of medium-sized LDCs.

In July 1984, Third World textile producers established an International Textiles and Clothing Bureau (ITCB) in Geneva to strengthen the negotiating position of developing countries through effective coordination and technical support. LDCs met in the spring of 1985 in Mexico City to coordinate a negotiating front. Significant differences among LDC textile and apparel producers made consensus difficult to achieve.

Most LDCs seek in principle a more liberal trading regime for textiles and clothing. The most competitive supplier–countries of East Asia prefer a "free-for-all" in world trade, although individual firms are willing to accept shares of the current import quotas.

LDCs that are internationally competitive in a few products generally prefer a mixture of free trade and restrictions. For example, India may support free markets for cotton products while it seeks guaranteed market access for other items.

The partially competitive and least competitive LDCs insist that their own uncompetitive textile and clothing sectors be protected and subsidized in order to promote development. Finally, the least competitive LDCs want to ensure their access to developed-country markets and may be willing to accept restrictive bilateral agreements that grant them market shares at the expense of major exporters.

In 1977 internal divisions had the LDCs in complete disarray from the outset of the renewal talks. In 1981 initial outward unity dissolved following U.S. and EC lobbying of individual LDC governments. LDCs completed work on a unified position for the 1985–86 renegotiation by exchanging information on individual bilaterals as well as relevant statistics that would allow for stronger MFA surveillance and enforcement. But a common overall position was difficult to formulate.

Public demands included elimination of the MFA and return to GATT rules for trade in textiles and clothing. Barring elimination of the MFA, many LDCs called for

progressive liberalization of quantitative import restraints;

development of a strict definition of "market disruption";

greater commitment to programs of long-term industrial adjustment in importing countries;

avoidance of globalization of import restrictions;

rapid removal of restrictions on cotton textiles;

protection of current access rights to developed-country markets;

greater international surveillance and enforcement regarding developed-country protectionism;

a floor under import growth rates; and

the right of LDCs to maintain selective barriers to textile and clothing imports.

DEVELOPED COUNTRIES' TEXTILE AND CLOTHING INDUSTRIES

For the developed-country members of the MFA, the late 1970s and early 1980s generally have been a period of stagnant or declining domestic demand for clothing and textiles. Depressed demand and increasing competition from exporting MFA countries have led to overall declines in output, employment, profits, the number of businesses, and trade balances. In Canada and the EC, production of textiles and clothing picked up in 1979 but then fell drastically during the 1981–82 recession. Japanese production in both sectors remained relatively stable from 1978 to 1982. Most developed countries experienced persistent negative trade balances in clothing and small positive balances in textiles through the late 1970s and early 1980s.

Government and business have attempted to counter the decline in the textile and clothing sectors. In the EC, private industry responses have included a move to industrial concentration in textiles and the reverse trend in clothing. The reasoning is that capital-intensive methods and economies on scale will lower the cost of textiles, whereas smaller units turning out specialized lines are advantageous in apparel production. EC textile and clothing producers have relied on investment in cost reduction and high-technology production methods, importation of low-cost foreign materials, overseas processing arrangements, and more aggressive exporting strategies.

Japanese industry characteristically has been able to strengthen its competitiveness in chosen textile and clothing categories by streamlining and upgrading production processes. The Japanese are adept at shifting capital and labor resources toward either specialized product lines or products where sophisticated mass production techniques bring improved international competitiveness.

DEVELOPED COUNTRIES AND THE MFA

Despite some success at so-called positive adjustments in the major European countries, Japan, and Canada, import restrictions have increased during the past ten years. The first MFA was more liberal than its predecessor, the LTA, because it allowed greater growth and flexibility in textile and clothing quotas. Following approval of the MFA, however, governments of importing countries imposed tighter limits on specific textile and clothing categories.

The EC strategy has been to seek a weak MFA regime that would allow the community to deal with LDC exporters on a bilateral basis without significant surveillance or enforcement. At the first MFA renewal in 1977, the EC threatened not to sign unless permitted to negotiate bilateral agreements allowing "reasonable departures" from MFA obligations. The reasonable departures clause was omitted from the 1981 protocol of renewal. But EC demands were satisfied partially by an antisurge clause designed to prevent domestic injury owing to sudden increases in imports from LDCs.

The EC's bilateral agreements with LDCs make up a complex, comprehensive system of quantitative restraints that apply to the whole range of MFA products. Restraints are placed on selected product categories for each exporting country. The largest number of restraints are found in agreements with East Asian suppliers. Japan currently has no formal quantitative limitations on imports from LDC members of the MFA. Since MFA I, Canada has negotiated a series of bilateral agreements with supplier countries. The agreements vary in terms of quota growth rates, flexibility, and category coverage, depending on the import sensitivity of domestic producers.

Most EC governments believe that their textile and clothing sectors still need the protective umbrella of the MFA and the MFA-sponsored bilaterals. EC concerns revolve around the disruptive imports of textiles and clothing from the principal low-cost LDC suppliers and the particular dangers provided by import surges in certain sensitive categories. The EC Commission developed an MFA negotiating position and recommended it to member nations in the summer of 1985. One of the hardline bargaining positions held certain import quotas constant and reduced imports from major LDC suppliers in favor of smaller suppliers.

The EC insisted that the United States and Japan share equally the burden of low-cost textile imports. They resisted assertions that the U.S. had taken a disproportionate share of 1983–84 surges in imports. They also insisted that their own recent slow import growth results from poor domestic economic performance and undervaluation of their currencies, which discourage imports from LDCs whose currencies are pegged to the U.S. dollar.

EC members appeared confident that some form of MFA IV would be approved in 1986. The Europeans believed that the LDCs would have little choice but to accept MFA renewal because market access would be at risk otherwise.

EC members' views on protection differed. The United Kingdom and France traditionally have supported stronger import restrictions, while West Germany, with an export-oriented clothing sector, is not as protectionist.

Because of its own history as an exporter of textiles, Japan generally has been opposed to restrictive use of the MFA. With a competitive textile industry and an expanding specialty clothing sector, Japan would prefer a fairly liberal regime, but its relative lack of direct involvement in the MFA system gave it a minor role in the bargaining process. Some developed countries called for

an MFA renewal for at least five years;

lowering the MFA minimum import growth rates below 6 percent per year in exceptional circumstances;

reduced flexibility for switching products between quota categories;

reduction of LDC tariffs, subsidies to domestic producers, and other barriers to developed-country exports; and

a liberalization of some aspects of the MFA.

WHICH DEVELOPED COUNTRIES ARE BEARING
THE GREATEST "BURDEN"?

The unity of developed countries at the MFA talks depended on perceptions regarding which countries were taking in the greatest share of LDC imports. Of the seven summit countries, the United States was by far the leading market for the ten largest clothing-exporting nations in 1983 (see Table 2.1). Measured in 1978–dollar value terms, the U.S. share was 57 percent of the summit countries' clothing imports from the major LDCs. West Germany took in 16 percent and Japan 11, while the United Kingdom, Canada, France, and Italy each took in less than 10 percent. Clothing import shares did not change significantly from 1978–83. The U.S. share increased by 3 percent over the period and the U.K. share lost 3 points.

Textile imports are more balanced. The United States leads with 34 percent; Japan accounts for 24 percent, and West Germany, 16 percent (in 1978–dollar value terms). The U.S. share is 8 points higher than it was in 1978. The increase came at the expense of the U.K. import share, which fell from 15 percent of the total to 9 percent, and the Japanese share, which fell from 29 to 24 percent. The U.K. decline in share reflected the absolute decline in U.K. imports from the ten LDCs. Japan increased imports during the six years, but not enough to prevent a fall in its textile import share.

Turning from import shares to import growth rates, France (15.2 percent) and Italy (10.2 percent) had the highest average annual growth rates of clothing imports in 1979–83, with 1978 the base year (see Table 2.2). These high rates are explained by surges in domestic consumer demand in 1979–80. Imports by these countries subsequently stagnated and even declined in constant dollar terms owing in part to the 1981–82 worldwide recession.

The United States has provided a more dependable clothing market than the other six countries, with imports growing at an average annual rate of 8.2 percent in 1979–83. Real imports grew at an accelerated rate from 1979–82 and ballooned in 1983 and 1984. (The growth rate for U.S. clothing imports from all coun-

Table 2.1
**Textile and Clothing Imports from the 10 Largest LDC Suppliers—
1978–83**
(billions of 1978 U.S. dollars)

	1978	1979	1980	1981	1982	1983	Total
Clothing							
U.S.	4.4	4.5	4.7	5.1	5.4	6.4	30.5
F.R.G.	1.4	1.5	1.8	2.0	1.9	1.8	10.4
Japan	.9	1.3	1.1	1.3	1.5	1.2	7.3
U.K.	.78	.86	.81	.90	.82	.77	4.9
Canada	.38	.39	.35	.40	.38	.48	2.4
France	.17	.25	.34	.39	.38	.33	1.9
Italy	.08	.10	.15	.16	.15	.12	.76
Textile							
U.S.	.19	.55	.66	.82	.70	.88	3.8
F.R.G.	.31	.36	.40	.41	.38	.43	2.3
Japan	.59	.80	.62	.65	.67	.64	4.0
U.K.	.31	.30	.22	.20	.21	.24	1.5
Canada	.07	.08	.07	.07	.06	.07	.42
France	.59	.80	.62	.68	.65	.62	4.0
Italy	.12	.17	.18	.18	.19	.18	1.0

Source: Data Resources, Inc.

tries in 1984 was 21 percent, calculated at 1978 prices.[3]) Japan's
clothing imports increased at a slightly faster rate than U.S.
imports in 1979–83. West Germany's relatively low average
growth rate of 5.5 percent would have been much higher except
for recession-caused stagnation in clothing import growth during 1982 and 1983. Canada's clothing import trends are closely
correlated with U.S. trends, although in 1979 and 1982 imports
declined in absolute terms.

Taken as a group, the seven summit countries experienced a
6.5 percent annual average growth rate of clothing imports in the
five-year period, compared with the 6 percent minimum rate
specified by the MFA.

U.S. textile imports fluctuated sharply around a trend rate of
11.8 percent. Italy's high average growth rate of 13 percent reflected an explosive 1979 jump of 57.4 percent. After 1979,

Table 2.2
Textile and Clothing Imports from the 10 Largest LDC Suppliers—
1979–83
(annual percentage growth rates)

	1979	1980	1981	1982	1983	Average
Clothing						
U.S.	1.8	4.4	9.9	4.3	20.0	8.2
F.R.G.	10.4	18.0	10.3	−11.2	1.1	5.5
Japan	4.5	−1.8	20.8	14.1	19.5	8.5
U.K.	11.2	−6.0	10.4	−8.4	6.3	0.2
Canada	4.3	−10.6	14.5	− 5.7	25.6	5.6
France	43.0	35.4	14.9	− 2.5	−13.3	15.5
Italy	21.3	48.2	5.1	− 2.9	−20.6	10.2
Textile						
U.S.	2.9	20.0	25.0	−14.0	25.1	11.8
F.R.G.	15.8	11.0	11.8	− 6.8	12.4	6.7
Japan	34.7	−22.8	5.3	4.1	−6.1	3.0
U.K.	−1.6	−26.0	−9.0	2.6	3.6	4.1
Canada	16.0	−14.6	9.6	−17.6	25.8	3.9
France	34.7	−22.9	5.3	4.1	6.1	3.0
Italy	57.4	7.3	−1.5	4.7	−2.9	13.0

Source: Data Resources, Inc.

growth of Italy's textile imports slowed considerably. Japan's textile imports have grown much more slowly than clothing imports as a consequence of a long-term adjustment from clothing production toward the capital-intensive textile sector.

West Germany's textile imports, which are mostly inputs for the large German clothing industry, grew at an average rate of 6.7 percent during the five-year period, falling only in the recession year of 1982. U.K. textile imports grew at a relatively low 4.1 percent per year because of depressed derived demand. Only in 1983 did U.K. textile imports expand briskly. Canada's textile imports rose and fell roughly at the same times as U.S. imports, but year-to-year changes were even more variable and fluctuated around a much lower average growth rate of 3.9 percent.

The industrial nations increased textile imports from the LDCs

Table 2.3
Import Penetration by the 10 Largest LDC Suppliers—1978–83
(ratios as percent)

Textiles	1978	1979	1980	1981	1982	1983
U.S.	1.2	1.3	1.6	2.0	1.9	2.1
Japan	1.8	2.3	1.8	1.8	1.9	1.8
F.R.G.	2.0	2.3	2.7	3.0	2.9	NA
U.K.	NA	3.3	3.2	NA	NA	NA
France	1.1	1.3	1.5	1.5	1.5	1.5
Italy	NA	1.4	1.5	NA	NA	NA
Canada	2.2	2.5	2.1	2.2	2.3	2.5

Note: Import penetration ratios: value of imports as a percentage of value of
      imports plus domestic shipments.

Source: Data Resources, Inc.

at an aggregate rate of 6.1 percent, compared with the MFA
minimum of 6 percent.

IMPORT PENETRATION IN DEVELOPED
COUNTRIES

Another measure of import burden is the so–called import
penetration (IP) ratio—imports of a product as a share of the
domestic market of the product. For most of the seven summit
countries, textile import penetration by the ten largest LDC suppliers is much lower than clothing import penetration (see Tables
2.3 and 2.4), reflecting the relative competitiveness of developed-country textile industries.

These IP ratios are much lower than the ratios sometimes
associated with developed-country textile and clothing imports.
The main reasons for the difference are

IP ratios calculated in value terms (Tables 2.3 and 2.4) can be as little as
50 percent of ratios calculated in physical (square-yard equivalent)

Table 2.4
Import Penetration by the 10 Largest LDC Suppliers—1978–83
(ratios as percent)

Clothing	1978	1979	1980	1981	1982	1983
U.S.	9.3	10.0	10.5	11.5	11.4	NA
Japan	6.9	9.6	8.1	8.9	10.1	7.9
F.R.G.	12.7	14.1	16.5	19.3	18.7	NA
U.K.	NA	16.9	19.1	NA	NA	NA
France	3.2	4.5	5.7	6.3	5.9	5.5
Italy	NA	2.1	3.0	NA	NA	NA
Canada	12.2	12.4	12.0	13.9	14.8	17.4

Note: Import penetration ratios: value of imports as a percentage of value of imports plus domestic shipments.

Source: Data Resources, Inc.

terms. Value-derived IP ratios are useful alternatives to physical unit ratios because they help account for quality differences between imports and domestic production.

The base group is the ten largest LDC suppliers, which may together provide only a small proportion of imports for the seven summit countries. Most IP calculations use total imports from all sources.

The IP ratio is defined as imports relative to potential total supply, or imports over domestic production plus imports. Another commonly cited definition measures imports relative to apparent consumption, or imports over domestic production plus imports minus exports. Because the apparent-consumption IP ratio subtracts exports from the denominator of the fraction, it will always be higher than the potential-supply ratio.

The United Kingdom's IP ratio was the highest, at 3.3 percent in 1979 and 3.2 percent in 1980, the only years for which U.K. data were available.[4] West Germany was second to the United Kingdom in 1980 and was first in 1981 and 1982. Canada generally had the next highest ratio, followed by Japan and the United States. France and Italy had the lowest ratios.

Textile IP ratios showed an upward trend in most of the developed countries. The ratio remained most stable in Japan, where domestic textile production grew significantly.

The U.S. IP ratio rose by 75 percent from 1978–83. West Germany's textile IP ratio increased almost as much as the U.S. ratio. A major factor was the decline in West German textile production, especially after 1980.

IP ratios for clothing follow a similar country ordering. The United Kingdom is first, with ratios about 17–19 percent, followed by West Germany, with ratios only slightly lower. Canada is third, followed by the United States with ratios about 10–11 percent, and Japan, with ratios near 10 percent. France (about 4–6 percent) and Italy (2–3 percent) had the lowest ratios.

Clothing IP ratios exhibited greater change over time than did textile ratios. This is caused by faster import growth for clothing and recent stagnant domestic production in the clothing industries of the seven summit countries.

From 1978 to 1982 France's clothing IP ratio almost doubled. While most of the increase reflected a 1979–80 import surge, declining domestic production throughout the entire period contributed to the IP increase.

The West German and Japanese IP ratios increased by almost 50 percent from 1978 to 1982. The U.S. IP ratio went up by almost 25 percent. As with textiles, generally positive growth in U.S. clothing production attenuated the effect of high import growth on the IP ratio.

WHICH LDCs HAVE HAD THE GREATEST ACCESS TO THE U.S. MARKET?

Textile and clothing trade between the United States and developing countries has been influenced by new protective measures and rising demand, as well as continued differences in production costs. The proliferation of U.S. import restrictions has slowed some LDC exports, and LDCs have strongly attacked the United States for shrinking their market access. Strong U.S. growth and a high dollar expanded import demand and dampened the criticism, however.

The three largest suppliers of clothing to the U.S. market in

Table 2.5
U.S. Clothing Imports From the 10 Largest LDC Suppliers—1978–83
(ratio of supplier country to all 10 supplier countries—ratios as
percent)

	1978	1979	1980	1981	1982	1983
Hong Kong	35	34	34	32	31	30
Taiwan	25	26	27	25	25	25
Rep. of Korea	24	22	21	22	21	22
China	2	4	6	8	11	11
Philippines	5	5	5	5	4	4
Indonesia	NA	NA	NA	1	1	1
Singapore	3	3	3	3	2	3
India	4	4	3	4	3	4
Pakistan	NA	1	1	1	1	1
Brazil	NA	1	1	1	1	1
Total	98	100	101	102	100	101

Note: NA means data were not available.

Source: Data Resources, Inc.

1983 were Hong Kong (30 percent), Taiwan (25 percent), and
South Korea (22 percent) (see Table 2.5).[5] China was next (11
percent), while the other six countries supplied less than 5 percent each. The 1983 shares are similar to those of 1978 except with
respect to China, whose share rose to 9 percent, and Hong Kong,
whose share fell 5 points.

Country shares for textile imports to the United States are
much more balanced (see Table 2.6). The leaders in 1983 were
South Korea (21 percent), China (19 percent), Taiwan (17 percent), and Hong Kong (13 percent). The biggest losses in shares
from 1978 to 1983 occurred for India (7 percentage points) and
Hong Kong (6 points). The biggest share gainers were South
Korea (10 points) and China (7 points).

Import figures assessed in absolute terms indicate the United
States is a huge and growing recipient of LDC clothing. Clothing
imports from the ten countries increased from $4.4 billion in 1978
to $6.4 billion in 1983 (1978 dollars), or by almost 50 percent.
None of the ten major LDC clothing suppliers had an average

Table 2.6
U.S. Textile Imports From the 10 Largest LDC Suppliers—1978–83
(ratio of supplier country to all 10 supplier countries—ratios as percent)

	1978	1979	1980	1981	1982	1983
Hong Kong	19	18	15	14	12	13
Taiwan	14	11	12	14	15	17
Rep. of Korea	11	10	15	16	20	21
China	12	11	17	21	22	19
Philippines	3	4	3	3	3	2
Indonesia	NA	NA	NA	NA	NA	1
Singapore	2	2	2	2	1	1
India	18	18	16	12	12	11
Pakistan	9	12	9	8	6	6
Brazil	11	14	11	8	8	9
Total	99	100	100	96	99	100

Note: NA means data were not available.

Source: Data Resources, Inc.

annual growth rate below 4 percent despite two recessions and a growing number of import restrictions (see Table 2.7).

The U.S. market accommodated particularly rapid growth of imports from three emerging clothing producers—China, Indonesia, and Pakistan. Indonesia's average growth rate for 1979–83 was 76 percent. After declines in 1979 and 1980, Indonesia's exports exploded during the next three years. Following Indonesia were China, with an average growth rate of 58 percent, and Pakistan, with 23 percent. China's year-to-year growth rates diminished throughout the period, partly reflecting the gradual imposition of bilateral restraints in major clothing categories and partly reflecting a rapid increase in the base for calculations. For all three countries, the growth of exports to the United States tracked overall rapid growth in domestic production of clothing.

Bilateral restraint agreements slowed clothing export growth for some established LDC suppliers. Hong Kong, Taiwan, South Korea, and Singapore had average growth rates of 7.3 percent or less. Growth would have been much slower were it not for the U.S. economic recovery and appreciating U.S. dollar. Also, these

Table 2.7

U.S. Clothing Imports From the 10 Largest LDC Suppliers—1979–83 (annual percentage growth rates calculated from 1978 dollar values)

	1979	1980	1981	1982	1983	Average Growth Rate
Hong Kong	1.6	3.1	4.8	1.3	13.6	4.9
Taiwan	3.3	10.2	− 0.5	8.1	15.6	7.3
Rep. of Korea	−6.0	−1.6	4.5	−.1	24.7	6.2
China (PRC)	120.7	57.5	52.9	39.8	20.7	58.3
Philippines	−.1	−2.2	12.7	−8.0	20.4	4.4
Indonesia	−40.9	−36.9	373.1	16.0	69.4	76.0
Singapore	−1.2	.1	.1	−1.3	27.9	5.4
India	3.9	−18.6	21.9	−9.9	33.8	6.2
Pakistan	52.6	−4.7	45.3	−3.1	26.2	23.3
Brazil	−31.4	−26.5	26.2	8.7	56.3	6.7

Source: Data Resources, Inc.

LDCs were able to expand clothing exports by increasing sales in categories not subject to specific quota restraints, by shifting to underutilized categories, and by raising prices on restrained products.

The United States has also provided substantial growth for the major LDC textile suppliers. Imports from the ten countries increased from $530 million in 1978 to $880 million in 1983 (1978 dollars), or by 67 percent. Growth of import volume was highly variable across countries and years. For most countries growth rates jumped significantly in 1983 as overall U.S. demand increased (see Table 2.8).

Over the five-year period, Indonesia was the growth leader (as it was in clothing). Starting from a very low 1978 base, Indonesia's textile exports grew at an average annual rate of 135 percent, calculated in 1978–dollar values. Indonesia was followed by South Korea with a growth rate of 29 percent; China, 26 percent; and Taiwan, 18 percent.

Despite a large gain in 1983 (32 percent), Hong Kong's average textile export growth rate was 5 percent in 1978 dollars, reflecting its continued shift away from textiles and toward-higher priced clothing production. India's textile exports to the United States

Table 2.8
U.S. Textile Imports From the 10 Largest LDC Suppliers—1979–83
(annual percentage growth rates calculated from 1978 dollar values)

	1979	1980	1981	1982	1983	Average Growth Rate
Hong Kong	3.5	0.3	.22	−27.1	32.0	4.7
Taiwan	−18.5	28.7	44.9	−6.9	39.6	17.6
Rep. of Korea	−.01	75.2	33.3	6.2	33.1	29.4
China	−8.9	85.0	57.3	−12.5	9.6	26.1
Philippines	13.9	7.7	9.4	−20.5	10.0	4.1
Indonesia	−20.9	80.8	206.2	−32.5	440.7	134.9
Singapore	20.1	13.3	14.0	−40.7	−44.0	−7.5
India	2.2	5.5	−3.2	−15.2	11.9	0.2
Pakistan	40.0	−12.0	18.0	35.0	20.0	6.0
Brazil	24.0	−5.0	−5.0	−15.0	36.0	7.0

Source: Data Resources, Inc.

hardly grew at all during the five–year period. Reasons include U.S. import restraints, heavy home industrial demand for textiles, and increasing demand for Indian textiles by other developed countries.

EXPECTATIONS WHEN THE MFA IS RETAINED

In its three incarnations the MFA has had several broad effects, including helping developed countries protect declining industries and enabling some of the less competitive supplier countries to gain ground against the major producers. MFA IV likewise will have important economic and political consequences including

upward pressure on prices of most clothing and some textile products in developing countries—especially in less expensive clothing categories;

slower positive adjustment of uncompetitive textile and clothing industries in the developed countries than would otherwise occur;

a negative impact on world economic growth, as the MFA continues to prevent maximum specialization in products for which countries have the greatest comparative advantage;

a "ratcheting" of protectionism as MFA IV further institutionalizes textile and clothing trade regulation; and

proliferation of bilateral restraints on the exports of poorer, emerging producer nations.

CONSEQUENCES OF A RETURN TO GATT RULES

If trade in textiles and clothing were ever to be brought under GATT, trade restrictions would consist of tariffs or quantitative restrictions imposed under specific GATT provisions and applied with the nondiscriminatory most-favored-nation principle. Some advocates of this proposal envision a transition period when existing restrictions would be dismantled gradually by:

eliminating underutilized quotas first;

enlarging existing quotas at progressively faster rates; and

requiring that from a specified date, any new quantitative restrictions meet the provisions of GATT Article XIX, which allows for emergency action on imports of particular products.

The key economic and political consequences of moving toward GATT probably would include:

large overall increases in LDC clothing production and exports;

declining clothing prices or, at a minimum, less rapid price increases;

declining clothing production in the developed countries, the extent of decline depending on the pace of automation and corporate strategies in reaction to increased LDC competition;

uncertain effects on developed-country textile industries; given the relative competitiveness of textiles, developed-country success might come to depend on the openness of LDC markets;

higher foreign exchange earnings and economic growth for some LDCs;

redistribution of production and exports among LDCs in line with changes in relative cost and stages of product cycles;

as the previously dominant LDC suppliers began to lose market shares to emerging suppliers, greater political discord among them could arise; and

increased challenges to uncompetitive LDC textile and clothing firms if full GATT provisions were applied to their countries' trade policies as well.

Indications proved correct that talks over the third renewal of the MFA were the most confrontational yet and that the debate would run along North-South lines. But both developed-country and LDC views hinted that the negotiating environment was primed for a renewal of the MFA. The EC pushed for renewal; the LDCs proliberalization unity crumbled. MFA renewal was accompanied by several substantive changes designed to mollify specific countries' concerns. For instance, LDCs insisted that the TSB be granted greater enforcement authority. The EC demanded lower quota growth rates and an enhanced antisurge mechanism for sensitive import categories.

In 1981, EC restrictionist demands regarding sensitive category imports threatened to convert the MFA into a U.S.-LDC agreement while the EC went its own way. Only U.S. mediation efforts helped assure renewal. But many EC governments view the United States as the more protectionist importer in 1985. They anticipate that pressure from Congress and industry will force the U.S. government to support renewal of a more restrictive MFA, prompting some of them to predict that this time the EC, rather than the United States, will take a relatively more liberal stance.

The MFA negotiating atmosphere was affected to some extent by serious discussions concerning a new multilateral trade round. Textile trade and clothing trade traditionally have been discussed separately from other trade issues. But some LDCs and Japan suggested that this time textiles and clothing be incorporated into other trade deliberations. Given their widely disparate trade policy priorities, the United States, the EC, and developing countries may have made implicit or explicit deals in order to make progress in their own areas of concern. For instance, it is thought developed countries chose to make concessions regarding market access for LDC textile and clothing exports in order to guarantee serious LDC participation in the new trade round.

APPENDIX

Current MFA Signatories

Argentina		
Austria	Hungary	Poland
Bangladesh	India	Portugal (for Macau)
Brazil	Indonesia	Romania
Canada	Israel	Singapore
China	Jamaica	Sri Lanka
Colombia	Japan	Sweden
Czechoslovakia	Republic of Korea	Switzerland
Dominican Republic	Malaysia	Thailand
Egypt	Maldives	Turkey
El Salvador	Mexico	United Kingdom
EC	Norway	(for Hong Kong)
Finland	Pakistan	United States
Guatemala	Peru	Uruguay
Haiti	Philippines	Yugoslavia

NOTES

1. See Appendix for a list of current MFA signatories.

2. The seven summit countries—Canada, France, the Federal Republic of Germany, Italy, Japan, the United Kingdom and the United States—are the major Western economic powers, which hold an annual economic summit.

3. This 1984 figure is in square yard equivalent (SYE) terms.

4. These IP ratios are similar to OECD/World Bank figures. For instance, OECD calculated a 1980 IP ratio for the United Kingdom of 2.9 percent for textiles from developing Asia and 2.0 percent from all newly industrializing countries.

5. Taiwan is included in these calculations (even though it is not in the MFA) because of its importance as a textile and clothing supplier to the United States.

3

Tropical Timber: New-Styled Commodity Agreement?

With tropical timber the third largest commodity in world trade and the market growing, producer and consumer countries have developed a commodity agreement and made it available for signature. Unlike most other international commodity agreements, the new agreement did not include price stabilization provisions. This was the first commodity arrangement to be completed since the conclusion of the sixth United Nations Conference on Trade and Development (UNCTAD VI) in June 1983. It signals a new direction for future commodity agreements.

International gatherings for decades have discussed issues relating to tropical timber. Today, world consumption of tropical timber is depleting accessible supplies. Tropical hardwoods have become one of the most important primary commodities for developing countries in terms of export earnings. At the same time, tropical forests have suffered from extensive cutting for fuel, and from slash-and-burn agricultural practices. International action therefore focuses on optimal timber utilization and on producing-country desire to control the use of forest resources in order to maximize benefits.

Only an estimated 4 percent of the world's tropical forests are properly managed. The research and information activities of the new International Tropical Timber Organization (ITTO) could provide long-term planning and conservation benefits for producing and consuming countries.

Preparatory talks on an international timber agreement began under UNCTAD auspices in 1976. After a lengthy series of meetings, representatives of countries that produce or import tropical timber finally agreed in November 1983 to form ITTO. Their agreement was opened for signature on January 2, 1984, and entered into force on October 1, 1984.

Unlike most other commodity agreements negotiated under UNCTAD auspices, this arrangement has no price stabilization provisions. Projects under the agreement depend on voluntary contributions or on future financing from the Second Window of the Common Fund. (The Common Fund is the centerpiece of UNCTAD IV's integrated program for commodities, and was designed to lend money to buffer stock operations of international commodity agreements.) Initial project financing is to come in the form of soft loans or grants from the United Nations Development Program (UNDP) and the World Bank. Administrative costs are divided according to a system based on net trade volumes.

MARKET CONDITIONS

Tropical timber follows oil and coffee in world trade value. The U.N. Food and Agriculture Organization (FAO) estimated a record world timber trade in 1979 of $8 billion. After 1979, timber sales fell off and did not begin to rebound until 1983.

Trade in tropical timber has expanded rapidly, if not continuously, over the last three decades. The main producers are

Asia-Pacific (India, Indonesia, Kampuchea, Laos, Malaysia, Papua New Guinea, the Philippines, the Solomon Islands, and Vietnam);

Africa (Cameroon, the Central African Republic, Congo, Gabon, Ghana, the Ivory Coast, Liberia, Nigeria, and Zaire); and

Latin America (Brazil, Colombia, Costa Rica, Ecuador, Paraguay, Peru, and certain Caribbean islands).

A World Bank study of prospects for major primary commodities forecasts slower growth in demand for tropical timber as well as problematic supply during the next 15 years. Currently Malaysia and Indonesia are by far the largest exporters of tropical timber, with 40 percent and 35 percent of the world total, respectively. The next most important exporting country is the Ivory

Coast, which has a 6.5 percent share of the market. Indonesia's processing industry is growing rapidly but is still relatively small. Indonesia also is expanding the manufacture of plywood. Brazil has the largest reserves, with an estimated tropical forest of 349 million hectares covering more than 60 percent of the country's area (mostly in the Amazon Basin). More than 400 species of commercial value have been identified, only 170 of which are used. Less than 20 percent of the wood that is cut reaches the world market. Brazil's current position in world trade is minimal.

At present, Japan imports 45 percent of the world's tropical timber, the European Community (EC) 30 percent, and the United States just under 10 percent.

THE U.S. MARKET

The U.S. market for tropical timber imports has grown with the rising needs of the building and furniture industries. Demand for hardwood plywoods especially has grown very rapidly over the last 20 years. Given the expected growth of the world economy and the elasticity of demand for tropical hardwoods, the outlook for the industry continues to be relatively bright. Supply-side constraints and higher prices mean growth of U.S. consumption probably will be slower, however, than the 6.7 percent annual increase in 1960–70 or even the 3.1 percent in 1970–80.

The structure of the tropical timber trade is changing. Although Southeast Asia has been the predominant U.S. supplier, Central and South America now are taking larger shares of the U.S. market because of restrictions on log exports from Indonesia, Malaysia, and the Philippines, South Korea, and Taiwan. Traditional suppliers in Asia, which in 1981 together accounted for more than 80 percent of total world exports, have reduced their exports through quotas or outright bans and by increased royalties, taxes, and other charges on log exports. Their objectives are to conserve resources, collect higher revenues, and expand the local processing industries. New supplies are expected to come from expanding production in countries that do not have strict export restrictions, including Burma, Papua New

Guinea, Equatorial Guinea, and the untouched forests of Ama-
zonia and Central Africa.

OBJECTIVES OF INTERNATIONAL TROPICAL
TIMBER AGREEMENT

For seven years UNCTAD held meetings involving tropical
timber producing and importing countries. Producing countries
themselves had longstanding internal disagreements over such
basics as the definition of "tropical timber." Asian producers
tried without success to broaden the definition beyond the four
eventually agreed product categories: logs, sawnwood, veneer,
sheets and plywood. For purposes of the agreement, "tropical
timber" finally was defined as "non-coniferous tropical wood for
industrial uses, which grows or is produced in the countries
situated between the Tropic of Cancer and the Tropic of Capri-
corn" (International Tropical Timber Agreement, 1984).

Concern over market instability eventually brought about a
convergence of commercial and ecological interests in tropical
woods. Prices were relatively stable prior to 1973, but since then
have varied by as much as 183 percent in a single year. Increases
in earnings have been more frequent, and greater than decreases. Uneven growth, therefore, rather than absolute decline,
has characterized the instability in export earnings from tropical
timber.

According to UNCTAD, producing countries are concerned
about structural, infrastructural, and technological deficiencies
in their timber industries. To overcome these problems, better
management and more extensive reinvestment, maintenance,
and preservation are needed on both short- and long-term bases.

Producing countries have for some time sought to lessen the
price fluctuations of tropical timber. In the early period of negotiations, UNCTAD sought price levels that would

be "remunerative" and "just" to producers and "equitable" to consumers;

take account of world information and the world economic situation;

promote short- and long-term equilibrium between supply and demand
within an expanding world trade;

maintain the quality of tropical timber;

ensure a more efficient use of resources, including the labor force;

support the establishment and continuation of tropical timber-based industries in producing countries; and

assure steady increases in the real income of producing countries.

Over a protracted period, price-control measures gradually were eliminated from the proposed commodity agreement because of their impracticality and resistance by importing countries. Unlike certain other commodities, logs deteriorate quickly; chemical treatment is both expensive and complicated. Thus perishability as well as the heterogeneous nature of the commodity militates against price stabilization through the use of buffer stocks. In the end, common interests of consumer and producing countries coalesced around the watered-down aims of the ITTO, as stated in Article I of the Agreement:

. . . to promote the expansion and diversification of international trade in tropical timber and the importance of the structural conditions of the tropical timber market, taking into account long-term interests in consumption and the availability of supplies and prices which are profitable for the producers and fair for consumers, as well as the importance of access to the market. (International Tropical Timber Agreement, 1984)

To accomplish these aims, the Agreement established three committees: Economic Information and Market Intelligence, Reforestation and Forest Management, and Forest Industry. Research and development is to be an implicit function of all three committees.

After lengthy discussions on the distribution of voting powers, agreement was reached on a formula that allocates ten votes per importing country and the balance to producing countries on the basis of trade shares. There is no upper limit for any single country. A portion of producing-country votes is based on forest resources. These are novel approaches to vote distribution not found in other international commodity agreements. The United States reserved endorsing the voting formula and special vote procedures.

Agreement has not yet been reached on location of ITTO

headquarters. As of 1986 seven countries had made offers: Belgium, France, Greece, Indonesia, Japan, the Netherlands, and the United Kingdom. Brazil was also said to be interested.

The United States still decided to become a signatory to the organization after much deliberation. Nearly every other large importing country, as well as every producing country, is expected to enter into the Agreement.

The passage of such a heterogeneous commodity through a series of intermediate processors, dealers, and distributors into a wide variety of end uses generates a large amount of information, much of which is not recorded. Complete market transparency would be impossible to achieve, but the ITTO will conduct studies on long-term trends in demand and supply. Accurate and constant information relating to market structure, conditions, and behavior will provide better estimates of wood value, existing resources, and growth potential, including forecasts and yield planning (particularly thinning treatments).

ITTO research grants could originate, jointly sponsor, or extend existing research and development projects. Likely topics for future projects include: research on forest management techniques; reinvestment; quality control; expansion of end uses; maximization of lesser used or lesser known species and of mill residues; promotional activities; rapid-growing species for fuel and paper; and processing in exporting countries to promote industrialization and reciprocal trade, including the opening of new markets, particularly in Africa.

Because the committees will only meet in person at membership meetings, the main permanent ITTO operating mechanism will be the executive secretariat and its staff. Speculation over the choice of a secretary general suggests that either a technical expert or an administrator familiar with UNCTAD will be named. Consuming countries generally favor the former.

The development of this first agreement since the conclusion of UNCTAD VI is noteworthy in itself. Other UNCTAD programs currently are in trouble. Even a small sucess would improve UNCTAD's somewhat negative image. Numerous benefits could result from an effective ITTO, including international standardization of species nomenclature, qualities, grades, and specifications of tropical timber. Reforestation and environmentally sound management programs could result in an expansion of renewable forests, which take from 40 years to more than 100 years to grow. ITTO could play an important role in improving knowledge of the tropical timber market and overcoming supply difficulties. The exchange of information among numerous national and regional bodies and the FAO Tropical Forest Development Committee is long overdue: Data could be exchanged on market conditions, rational forest utilization and management, timber processing, handling procedures, transport methods, and research and development.

Japan's involvement in ITTO provides an additional forum for the United States to address bilateral trade-related problems. This forum might prove useful for discussions not only of tropical timber, but also of related products.

For years, environmental and industry groups have supported the idea of a tropical timber organization, although for differing reasons. Because the agreement that has been worked out does not have any price-fixing mechanism, it is a prime example (like the one for jute) of an "other measures" agreement. Such an arrangment does not attempt to set price guidelines for a commodity; rather, it seeks to improve factors affecting international trade.

Of course the producers hope such an agreement will further their long-term aim of increasing their earnings. Whether the timber agreement will be widely accepted as a prototype for other commodities will depend on interested parties' (1) willingness to devote years of preparation to agreements whose benefits are diffuse and impossible to quantify, and (2) realization that each "other measures" agreement will have to be tailored to the specific commodity under consideration.

4

Lome III: To Be or Not To Be?

Renegotiation of the Lome Agreement between the European Community (EC) and the African, Caribbean, and Pacific (ACP) group of developing countries was completed in February of 1985. The Lome pact defines EC economic relations with the Third World and furthers an important trade relationship for both parties.

This chapter argues that the initially innovative Lome arrangement has proven to be a disappointment to both sides. Reservations over performance have led some EC governments to question the viability of the restrictive Lome arrangements, while ACP countries have complained about lack of funding for development programs.

It is probable that the achievement of Lome III will be less than satisfactory to its contracting parties, especially to the ACP countries. U.S. trade concerns will be relatively unaffected by Lome III, although EC-ACP relations and development schemes continue to interest U.S. policymakers. The Lome Agreement of 1985 could, according to some commentators, be the end of the EC's restrictive regional approach to development because of its cost and discrimination against other LDCs.

Formal negotiations between the EC and the ACP involving some 64 LDCs over a successor agreement to the second Lome Convention (which expired February 28, 1985) commenced in October 1983 (see Table 4.1). For nearly three decades, negotiated conventions have been the centerpiece of EC policy toward the Third World. The fixed five-year duration of the two earlier

Table 4.1
ACP Agregate STABEX Transfers by Commodity
(by percentage)

Product	Percentage
Ground nuts	19.03
Ground nut oil	18.15
Iron ore	16.48
Cotton	11.57
Roughwood	10.19
Sisal	5.49
Oil cakes	4.42
Coffee	3.87
Raw hides and skins	2.24
Tea	2.23
Palm nut and kernel oil	1.23
Bananas	0.78
Vanilla	0.77
Palm oil	0.60
Copra	0.58
Coconut oil	0.56
Cloves	0.30
Cocoa	0.28
Ground nut oil cakes	0.27
Gum Arabic	0.23
Sawnwood	0.19
Palm nuts and kernels	0.17
Pyrethrum	0.16
Cocoa paste	0.12

Source: ACP-EC Consultative Assembly

Lome Conventions, the Yaounde Conventions predating them, and the various association agreements that preceded Yaounde, have involved the EC at regular intervals in review and renewal of relations with key Third World nations and trading partners. Renewals of the original 1958 EC-ACP agreements have taken place in 1963, 1969, 1975, and 1979, and the latest renewal of 1985.

COOPERATION AND INTERDEPENDENCE

Cooperation with the Third World is a vital economic necessity for nations that comprise the EC.[1] Europe, like Japan, but to a greater extent than other developed-country trade groupings or regions, is dependent on the Third World for energy, raw materials, and markets. Questions of development and interdependent Third World relations therefore have generally been accorded a higher profile for the EC than they have for most other developed states.

The EC inherited a colonial relationship with much of the Third World that predetermined its trade patterns. As colonialism receded, the EC fostered new relationships with many of the Third World countries that continued to provide secure and competitively priced supplies of raw materials, markets for manufactured goods, and opportunities for investment.

The EC transformed the largely French programs of the 1960s into the economic agreements of the Yaounde Conventions, which maintained preferential access to the sources of raw materials and Western European markets in return for financial and technical assistance and foreign aid.[2] (By value, 99.5 percent of ACP exports now enter the EC duty-free.) This, combined with development aid from the European Development Fund (EDF), the rights of establishment and free movement of labor between European and associated areas, set the stage for all future EC-ACP agreements. The EC dependence on the Third World, a desire to spread influence and culture, as well as longstanding humanitarian concerns, resulted in the 1970s in a more ready acceptance by Europeans of arguments for interdependence articulated in the North-South dialogue.

The four formally articulated fundamentals of Lome policy have been:

1. Dependable cooperation based on a system of entitlement in a freely negotiated contract between equal partners.
2. Respect for an individual country's nonalignment, national and cultural independence.

3. Global definition of needs in light of the priorities of ACP countries and their levels of development.

4. Permanent dialogue, ensured by institutional structures that can bring about a widening scope of consultations.

When the time for renewal of the convention came in 1979, the EC, suffering from internal problems, questioned the effectiveness of Lome I, but its member governments found themselves unwilling to undertake major changes in the existing arrangements. ACP members, on the other hand, expressed disillusionment and dissatisfaction with the convention, but were not sufficiently organized or united to bring about what they alleged were "necessary reforms." As a result, Lome II was largely a continuation of Lome I with very few new initiatives.

A CHANGING WORLD

Between 1979 and 1984 significant changes in the global economy occurred that affected EC relations with the Third World. Economic recession had a major negative effect on the economies of all EC member states. Unemployment has been exceptionally high by historical standards. The political complexion of Europe has changed since 1975. The EC countries have adopted stringent economic policy measures to adjust to the new realities. Protectionist tendencies have by-and-large been checked within the EC itself, but the Community has demonstrated increasing protectionism in its dealings with the rest of the world. Because EC governments are closely scrutinizing policies for cost effectiveness, the Lome Convention (as well as other trade and aid agreements) was more sharply inspected than in the past.

Simultaneously, Third World countries have experienced an economic crisis that they say is of unprecedented proportions. Some developing countries have also been affected by what they view as nearly insurmountable debt problems. Many LDCs have simply been unable to sustain their long-term development efforts. Slumping prices for commodities, oil price increases in 1973 and 1979, inflation, and intense competition have had an impact on most developing countries.

During this time period many people have questioned the effectiveness of the Lome Conventions, thereby challenging the foundations of one part of the European perspective on the North-South dialogue.

Academic experts, government and trade officials, and even the recipient developing countries themselves, are increasingly critical of and frustrated with the Lome arrangements. EC governments have come to wonder if the Convention is worth its cost. The Europeans are also being pressed by nonassociated Third World countries and by the GATT to drop preferential agreements altogether. Moreover, trade with non-ACP developing countries has become increasingly more important to the EC. Since the ACP includes 25 of the 31 poorest countries in the world, many of these countries offer little to their European partners.

PIECEMEAL POLICIES TOWARD THE THIRD WORLD

The EC does not have a comprehensive or systematic policy on Third World development. Instead, the Community has a variety of policies, agreements, and arrangements that have grown up over time in a piecemeal fashion. Decisions on foreign trade are made at the Community level rather than by member states independently. EC member states have also functioned as a group in international economic forums dealing with trade matters, and conclude trade agreements through the medium of the Community.

The Common Agricultural Policy (CAP) is one key mechanism the Community uses to influence policy toward the Third World. The CAP was designed to promote a profitable European agricultural sector and to pursue a degree of agricultural self-sufficiency for the EC through extensive protection against import competition, while allowing importation of agricultural products that do not compete with items produced in Europe.

The EDF has supplemented development efforts by financing investments aimed at increasing production and improving infrastructure, as well as social investments designed to build school and hospital facilities. Infrastructure projects have accounted for about 70 percent of allocated funds. Historically, only 6 percent of EDF funds have been devoted to industrialization projects. EDF sectoral operations by allocations in ranked order of importance include

transport;

communication;

rural development;

education and training;

water engineering;

urban infrastructure;

industrialization;

health;

exceptional aids;

trade promotion; and

tourism.

INNOVATIONS MIXED WITH DISAPPOINTMENTS

Major innovations in the Lome Conventions included abandonment of the principle of reciprocity in trade, introduction of a special protocol on sugar, increased technical and financial cooperation by the EDF on development projects, and a concessionary export earnings stabilization scheme for important commodities (STABEX). (STABEX funds were exhausted in 1980 and 1981.) By 1979, and the signing of the second Lome accord by 58 (currently 64) ACP member states, the atmosphere was appreciably less positive. Both parties were disappointed by the results of association. The ACP states were concerned that Lome II was not a step forward, and even more so by the unilateral decisionmaking process. The EC, on the other hand, was frustrated by the extreme demands of the ACP and the lack of understanding of their own financial constraints given the damaging effects of the global economic recession.

The single innovation of Lome II was a system for maintaining or rehabilitating existing production capacity in ACP mineral industries. The need for this system had been evidenced by a significant drop in minerals production or export earnings.[3] The new system (SYSMIN), however, was less comprehensive than the previously instituted STABEX. Since SYSMIN is not automatically triggered, it is not available in the form of free foreign exchange for general budgetary purposes, nor does it promote new investment in mining projects.

Lome II has been under fire since its inception. Criticized by global trade organizations and non-ACP developing countries as either a selective extension or a derogation of the generalized system of preferences (GSP), Lome has been called "discriminatory." Some radicals have even suggested that Lome is a neo-colonial device to continue dependency and weaken Third World solidarity. Many economists have analyzed Lome data on performance and found the association wanting.

The direction of trade between ACP countries and EC countries over the last decade has been determined by relatively few countries. Nigeria, because of its oil production, alone accounts for 25 percent of ACP exports to the community. Presently the eight most important ACP exporters are Nigeria, Ivory Coast, Zaire, Cameroon, Kenya, Ghana, Zambia, and Gabon, who together account for 70 percent of the ACP's exports to the EC. During the last decade the ACP countries have not been able to maintain their market shares for primary products in the EC and failed to open up new markets for their manufactures. The duty-free access to the Community granted to the ACP signatories failed to achieve its overall objectives (Table 4.2).

RESERVATIONS ABOUT INCREASED COMMITMENTS

Faced with economic uncertainties and unresolved EC budgetary and financial problems, some EC governments entered the most recent renegotiations for a successor to Lome II with grave reservations about their ability to increase commitments to development aid, and with a realistic attitude about the effectiveness and viability of the restricted Lome arrangements. Some EC countries were even said to want to let Lome expire or to transform Lome into a truly global development policy.

Since the Lome Convention is still the centerpiece of EC rela-

Table 4.2
Twenty–Five Most Important Commodities
in ACP Exports

1. Petroleum	10. Cotton	19. Tobacco
2. Coffee	11. Thorium	20. Raw skins and
3. Cocoa	12. Tea	hides
4. Refined copper	13. Uranium	21. Diamonds
5. Oil derivatives	14. Aluminum oxide	22. Copper ore
6. Roughwood	15. Ground nut oil	23. Calcium
7. Sugar	16. Sawnwood	phosphates
8. Iron ore	17. Bananas	24. Cobalt
9. Blister copper	18. Aluminum ore	25. Natural rubber

Source: European Community.

tions with the developing world, its quick demise was not likely. Lome continues to exist alongside some 30 bilateral and multilateral agreements that together regulate the EC's trading links with LDCs.

The accession of Spain and Portugal to the EC does not bode well for EC–Third World relations. The lower level of development in Greece, Spain and Portugal, as well as the climatic conditions in this region, mean that these countries will provide, within the customs union, agricultural and semiprocessed products that could preempt importation of similar products from the developing countries. ACP states have already expressed concern on this point. The developing countries have also continually reminded the EC of their view that the impact of adverse global economic conditions on the developed countries has been minor compared to the problems experienced in the LDCs.

ACP terms of trade have continuously deteriorated and ACP states have been losing EC market shares to non-ACP countries in Latin America and Asia.[4] Trade volumes between EC and ACP countries have increased between 1970–84 but not as much as EC trade with non-ACP developing countries. Moreover, imports to the EC from the ACP are now dominated by a few countries.[5] ACP countries have also become more frustrated by the lack of progress toward industrialization and are upset over the EC's resort to safeguard clauses to protect the European market against processed goods, especially textiles, from the ACP countries.

Lome's focus on industrialization is recognized by both parties as minimal. The Center for Industrial Development (CID), created by Lome I, has lacked "operational content" and its funding remains rather limited. Concern over declining investment in ACP countries is well founded as investors have been cautious over risks, such as political instability and the possibility of nationalization. Even STABEX, the original cornerstone of Lome, was seriously questioned. According to some critics, the export earnings facility's laudable beginnings have not over time addressed meaningfully the problem of commodity earnings. Selective coverage limits (see Tables 4.1 and 4.2), inadequate financial transfers, and disincentives to ACP diversification make STABEX contributions somewhat dubious, according to its many detractors.[6]

THE PROCESS OF RENEGOTIATION

Both sides sought for a new convention that would foster self-reliant development in the ACP, with rural development the key to economic growth.[7] Negotiations commenced, despite rankling resentments, in October of 1983. EC decisions to encourage domestic sugar production, stifle imports of Kenyan strawberries, and attempt to cut existing ACP beef quotas did not help the negotiating environment. The Community position on Lome III stressed continuity and failed to incorporate much fresh stimulus for development. ACP countries, however, wanted more innovation.

The discussions were much less than euphoric. From January to April 1984 some points of convergence became apparent on trade, rules of origin, mining, energy, STABEX, aid, and industrial cooperation issues. The level of funding for the EDF has remained virtually untouched, to the ACP countries' dismay. The effects of EC enlargement to include Spain and Portugal were not negotiated. Some points of divergence were resolved at the ministerial meeting held in Fiji in May 1984, but what was to be the concluding session at Luxembourg, in June 1984, did not produce final texts. One concession was granted to ACP countries; namely, access to available (that is, surplus) EC agricultural products, albeit within existing EC rules and international obligations.

A final negotiating meeting in July failed to resolve outstanding issues, and yet another meeting was held in early October. New negotiating demands were tabled by the ACP group, which reopened some issues the EC side considered resolved. On October 12 the talks collapsed because the ACP rejected EC compromise proposals to overcome plaguing divisions, thereby placing the December 7 deadline in jeopardy. At the adjournment of the meetings, Community failure to finalize details was still evident. The ACP stated that the total aid package, whose present value is less than $6 billion measured in U.S. dollars, was too low, and smaller than the Lome II aid package in real terms.

Some of the most contentious issues concerned

structure and length of the convention (open ended or time limited);
food aid;
access to EC market for ACP agricultural products;
origin regulations;
extension of SYSMIN extension to include nickel and other minerals;
human rights;
fishing rights;
protection of EC investments in ACP states; and
sociocultural cooperation.

EC members themselves remain divided on the level of aid funding, with some members wanting to maintain Lome II levels (5.5 billion ECUs), some calling for 7.5 billion, the president of the EC council suggesting 8.2 billion, and the ACP states demanding that 10 billion ECUs is barely enough to carry out their aims.[8] The final outcome of funding for Lome III was at a level less than satisfactory to the ACP states.

Special efforts aimed at food security, boosting the food production of the ACP countries, and long-term campaigns for the conservation and exploitation of natural resources were part of the new Lome agreement. EDF Commissioner Pisani says he wanted to emphasize food, not "cathedrals in the desert." Reflecting interest in food security, Lome III witnessed the inclusion of provisions on the control of both drought and desertification. The new accord that emerged also addressed human rights questions; for example, the topic of EC relations with South Africa was part of the negotiations.

Protocols on bananas and rum remain much the same in the new convention despite the ACP request for abolition of quotas on rum. There was a new convention on rice, and ACP beef and veal quotas were raised. Lome III came about due to a ministerial meeting that broke key impasses and allowed the accord to be signed (in Lome) in early December 1984. But Lome III does not differ greatly from Lome II in substance, with the following exceptions: the concept of "policy dialogue" is more explicit in the new convention; there has been some beefing up of suggestions on investment; a declaration on social and culture cooperation was attached, and an emphasis on self-reliance and food security, as has been mentioned, was finally included.

The improvement of EC trade relations with other developing regions means that Lome III could, as some have suggested, serve as the finale to the EC's restrictive regional approach to development. Because of Lome's disappointing record and the clamor of other developing countries to end the discriminatory system of preferences, Lome's future is even more clouded than ever. It appears as though there was to be a Lome III and that its overall significance could be even less than its predecessor trade agreements. (The final differences were even worked out before the expiration of Lome II.) In spite of its record however, the EC appears willing to give the Lome experiment a longer trial.

From the U.S. point of view, the EC has clear economic reasons to maintain a trade advantage (measured in market shares) with the ACP countries. U.S. exports to the ACP have been declining compared to the pre-Lome period, whereas ACP exports to the United States have climbed dramatically in the same time period. The result is a U.S. balance-of-trade deficit with ACP states as a group that is not likely to change in the immediate future. One reason for continued EC-ACP economic stimulation is Lome. ACP states have also been, and are likely to remain, much more important to European investors than their U.S. counterparts because of historic, cultural and economic links.

NOTES

1. Ellen Frey-Wouters, *The European Community and the Third World: The Lome Convention and its Impacts*, (New York: Praeger, 1980).

2. European Community/ACP, "Lome Disaster," *The Courier*, No. 31, March 1, 1975.

3. Stevens, Christopher, *EEC and the Third World*, (London: Overseas Development Institute, 1984); Long, Frank, (ed.), *The Political Economy of EEC Relations with ACP States*, (New York: Pergamon, 1980); and Ross, J. and Ravenhill, J. "Trade Developments During Lome," *World Development*, vol. 10, October, 1982, pp. 841–56.

4. O'Shaughnessy, Hugh, "Europe and Latin America," *Europe*, No. 238, 1983; pp.34–35.

5. Ginsberg, Roy Howard, "The European Community and the Mediterranean," in Juliet Lodge, (ed.), *Institutions and Policies of the EC*, (New York: St. Martin's, 1983); and Ravenhill, John, "What is to be Done for Third World Commodity Exports?" *International Organization*, vol. 38, Summer 1984, pp. 537–74.

6. Moss, Joanna, *The Lome Conventions and Their Implications for the United States*, (Boulder, CO: Westview, 1982).

7. Noelke, Michael, *Europe and the Third World*, (Brussels: EC Commission, 1979).

8. Mahler, Vincent, "Britain, the EC and the Developing Commonwealth," *International Organization*, vol. 35, 1981, pp. 467–92; and Rajana, C. "Lome Conventions: An Evaluation of EEC Assistance to ACP States," *Modern African Studies*, vol. 20, June 1982, pp. 179–220.

5

LDC Steel Production and Capacity: Past Growth and Future Trends

Steelmaking capacity in the less developed countries (LDCs) continues to grow, furthering the trend toward self-sufficiency and export orientation in newly industrialized countries (NICs) and in countries where the steel industry is subsidized.[1] Crude steel capacity in LDCs could grow by 7 percent annually to 121 million metric tons (mmt) in 1986, from 93 mmt in 1981, despite the delays caused by the recent recession (see Appendix).

Crude steel capacity in the developed countries is projected to decline from 571 mmt to 555 mmt over the same period. Communist countries (except China and North Korea) are expected to increase their steelmaking capacity to 330 mmt in 1986, from 305 mmt in 1981. In 1985 the developed noncommunist countries are projected to have 55.1 percent of world steelmaking capacity (the United States having 13.4 percent); the LDCs, 12.1 percent; and the communist countries, 32.8 percent.

Disruption of the world steel market will be caused partly by the strengthening position of the LDCs and certain NICs. Projected developments include:

LDCs met as much as 90 percent of their own steel needs by 1986, compared with 60 percent in 1977;

LDCs may account for all of the net steel capacity expansion in the noncommunist world through 1990;

LDCs will import progressively less steel from the developed countries;

a 50 percent decline from the 32 mmt imported in 1977 took place by
1985;

Such NICs as Brazil, South Korea, South Africa, and Taiwan will export
increasing amounts of steel;

many LDC governments will maintain their sizable control over and
subsidization of national steel industries;

NIC competition will make recovery of OECD steel industries more
difficult; and

steelmaking in many developed countries probably will focus increasingly on rolling and finishing imported feedstock.

The economic geography of world steel production has
changed markedly. Moderate increases in total output and shifts
of production to the LDCs will continue.[2] Some of the changes in
steelmaking capacity during 1981–85 (in million metric tons)
were

Decreases		Increases	
U.S.	6.4	Latin America	14.7
Japan	3.6	Brazil	8.7
EC	10.0	Mexico	3.8
West Germany	2.9	Africa	3.1
United Kingdom	2.9	Nigeria	2.4
Belgium	2.1	Middle East	2.0
		Saudi Arabia	0.9
		Far East	16.0
		China	7.1
		India	1.7
		South Korea	3.2
		Taiwan	2.2
		USSR	13.6
		Eastern Europe	3.2

The LDCs have increased steel output more than fivefold since
1960. Larger NIC producers have become important steel exporters, taking markets from the Japanese, European, and U.S.
steel industries.[3] Steel has been designated by many LDCs as an
industry necessary for industrialization and economic develop-

ment. LDC leaders have argued that modern steel plants would give developing countries:

economic growth at low cost;

employment for skilled and semiskilled workers;

protection from price and supply instability;

stronger trade balances and;

symbols of improved national status.

A target for LDC steel production of 25 percent of the world total by 1990, suggested by the UN Industrial Development Organization (UNIDO) 1975 Lima Declaration, may be overly ambitious.[4] Yet some LDCs have continued a rapid expansion of their steel industries. In particular, Brazil, South Korea, and Taiwan are building large, integrated, export-oriented steel industries.

GROWTH OF LDC STEEL INDUSTRIES

LDC steelmaking capacity in the early 1960s was less than 10 mmt, only 3 percent of total noncommunist world capacity. LDCs imported 60 percent of their more than 20 mmt of annual steel consumption. Much of the steel they produced was of poor quality.

Ambitious expansion projects began during the late 1960s with government participation and international financial support, and LDC capacity grew dramatically. The newer LDC steel mills were modern, fully integrated plants incorporating the best engineering and services available and, thus, producing steel suitable for global markets. Even through the recessionary years of the 1970s, LDCs accelerated their steelmaking capabilities, although efficiency of the mills was sometimes decreased by poor managerial and production skills or inferior infrastructure. Joint ventures with firms from developed countries often provided the necessary capital and technology.

Effective capacity in the LDCs grew to 42 mmt in 1973, 8.5 percent of the noncommunist world total, and to 111 mmt in

1983, an estimated 11.4 percent of the total (see Figure 5.1). Some steel industry analysts believe LDC crude steel capacity in 1988 could be 121–36 mmt, representing 12.1–12.9 percent of the world total. Of course, much of the increase in LDC steel production is being consumed in the LDCs themselves. Global steel consumption increased by only 3 percent in 1973–83, decreasing in developed countries by 14 percent, but increasing by 53 percent in the LDCs. Future steel consumption is expected to grow twice as fast in developing countries as in developed countries.

World output of crude steel rose 2.9 percent in 1983, according to the International Iron and Steel Institute. Global production totaled 664 mmt, 19 mmt more than in 1982, but this growth still was the third smallest in the past decade. Leading industrial democracies increased their output 1.6 percent to 343 mmt, while the developing countries (excluding China) boosted their total by 5.4 percent, to 71 mmt.

Brazil's steel production jumped 12.8 percent in 1983 to nearly 15 mmt, while Taiwan's went up 20.5 percent to 5 mmt. Brazil, India, Mexico, South Africa, and South Korea now account for 71 percent of LDC steel capacity. Argentina, Taiwan, Venezuela, Iran, and Egypt—produce an additional 17 percent. All of these except India, Iran, and Egypt are increasing production and exports rapidly. The steel trade balance of the seven fast growers swung from 13 mmt net imports to 13 mmt net exports in less than ten years. The target capacity of these countries is 66 mmt by 1987, an increase of more than 4 percent per year over their 57 mmt in 1983.

Some 75 other LDCs, experiencing various degrees of financial and economic difficulties, also are engaged in steel production. Although their production has risen by nearly 50 percent since 1974, their net imports also have risen. These countries account for only 5 percent of the noncommunist world's steel production. The steelmaking capacity of this group will increase to 42 mmt by 1987.

Steel production in a developing country tends to grow steadily once it reaches an annual level of 300,000–500,000 mt. This is probably the minimal size of a viable steel industry. Expansion projects are under way in 32 LDCs, and numerous other LDCs have plans to expand.

Figure 5.1
Percentage of
World Crude Steel Production:
1960 to 1983

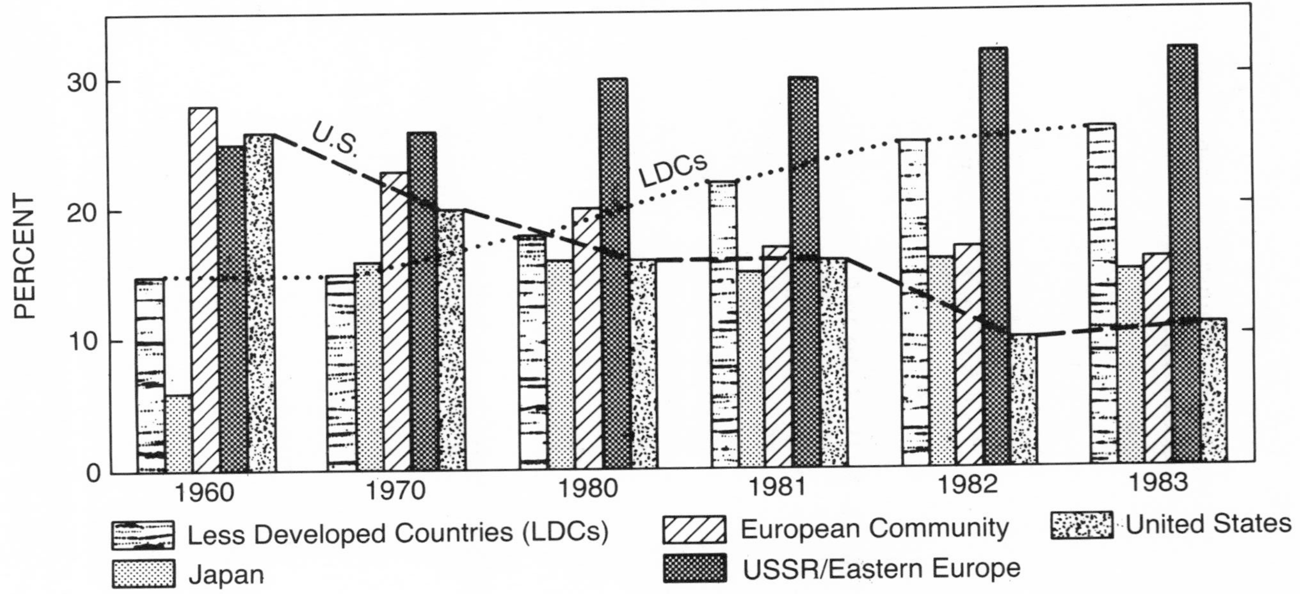

At least five factors affect the expansion of steel industries in developing countries:

1. Size of the domestic market.
2. Protection of the domestic market.
3. Availability of financing—including subsidization—for the industry.
4. Technological assistance and the supply of advanced technologies, operating know-how, and capital equipment.
5. Attitudes to regulation in potential importing countries.

GOVERNMENT OWNERSHIP

The state owns two-thirds or more of the typical LDC steel industry; the remainder is owned by foreign participants or private domestic investors. By one account, 22 integrated steel mills with an annual capacity of about 1 mmt each were operating in the LDCs in 1982, and all but 3 were state owned. Most private companies are small mills whose activity is confined to scrap smelting and production of reinforcing bars and light structures.

Private firms had only about 32 percent of Brazil's 18 mmt annual capacity in 1982. The figure is dwindling as state-owned facilities expand. Mexico's steel industry is 74 percent state owned despite a recent scaling down of ambitious expansion projects. Pohang Iron and Steel, a state-owned company, accounts for nearly 75 percent of South Korea's capacity, and the percentage will rise when a new mill (3 mmt annual capacity) becomes operational in 1988.

Sound economic performance is seldom a primary criterion in establishing a steel complex. The state-owned steel mills of most LDCs, other than South Korea and Taiwan, have incurred huge losses. These mills usually enjoy heavy subsidies and protection against foreign competition. Problems include

the high cost of plants and imported technology;

inadequate funding;

insufficient scale;

vast state bureaucracies;

lack of skilled workers; and

inability to make high-grade steel products.

FINANCING FACILITIES

The return on capital usually has been low in the steel industry because investment in steel has been greatly motivated by objectives other than profit. Many LDC governments have heavily supported site acquisition, infrastructure development, and provision of utilities. Further costs for protection against imports at the infant stages of industrial development (which tend to last indefinitely) often are passed on to taxpayers and consumers. Steel industries in most LDCs, with the notable exception of certain NICs, are characterized by cyclical behavior, moderate-to-huge operating losses, and dependence on government support and/or protection.

While the developed world is reducing steel capacity, LDCs are continuing to invest in new plant and equipment. Brazil has invested more than $16 billion in building new facilities and modernizing existing ones since 1978. The mammoth new Tubarao plant in Espirito Santo, a joint venture undertaken by the Brazilian firm Siderbras and Japanese and Italian companies, recently began producing 6 mmt annually, of which approximately 50 percent is exported. Final cost of the first phase of the plant is estimated at more than $2 billion. The 1.3-mmt Soviet-built plant at Ajakuto, Nigeria, is far behind schedule, may never be fully operational, and will cost almost double the original estimate.

LDC steel industries have been aided over the years by international lending institutions, the USSR, and the Organization of Petroleum Exporting Countries (OPEC). They also have obtained financial support on commercial terms from major banks and steel companies in the developed countries. U.S. banks, firms, and government have participated in loans and guarantees for financing steel projects in 46 countries since 1945.

In recent years the United States has prodded other industrialized countries to reduce export guarantees and concessionary loans for the construction of steel mills in the Third World with little success. Austria and Japan have opposed plans to limit low-interest loans and loan guarantees by official export credit banks. Britain has been less than enthusiastic about any pact. The OECD Steel Committee and Export Credits Group have fostered no multilateral agreement to restrict financing of new steel plants and equipment.[5]

Although slowed economic growth, balance-of-payments problems, and difficulty in obtaining financing threaten some new LDC steel projects, financing has been arranged for many now planned. Oil-exporting LDCs generally have had fewer financial restraints. India and Nigeria (an oil exporter with serious financial problems) have negotiated some financing from the Soviet Union. Brazil and China, among others, have found it difficult to finance all of their planned expansions.

TECHNOLOGY AND RAW MATERIALS

Most LDC steel mills use the direct-reduction method rather than the older blast furnace technology. South Korea is arguably the most efficient LDC producer, with facilities rivaling even the best in Japan. South Korea recently acquired advanced scanning auger systems to improve its higher-grade steelmaking capabilities. India and Nigeria have inefficient steel facilities.

A breakthrough in steel technology may be in the offing for minimills using electric furnaces to produce steel from scrap. Improvements in continuous casting would permit many LDCs to make efficiently flat-rolled steel products used in autos, appliances, storage drums, and roofing. Minimills serving local markets already enjoy advantages of lower capital costs and transportation. Steel analysts say a 100,000-ton minimill could be built with electric furnaces, continuous casting, and the necessary rolling mill for $200 million—an amount many LDCs could afford. Nucor, the most successful U.S. minimill company, predicts a revolutionary breakthrough in flat-rolling within the next few years. LDCs could benefit enormously from the rapid transfer of such technology.

The manufacture of steel requires large supplies of energy,

limestone, and such alloying elements as nickel, chrome, tungsten, cobalt, manganese, vanadium, and molybdenum—some of which come from such politically sensitive areas as southern Africa and the USSR. Although the phasing out of open hearths has lowered energy requirements, most LDC plants operate at low levels of energy efficiency. And only 14 LDCs have coke or coal reserves of any magnitude. Many LDCs likely will continue to use noncoke coals or formed coke, and will install electric arc furnace capacity more than the developed countries.

Most forecasters are predicting that world steel consumption and production will grow 1–3 percent annually through the entire 1980s. These forecasts assume different rates of economic growth, steel intensity, and energy availability, but all concur that growth of LDC output will continue to exceed that of world steel production: LDCs likely will account for all of the net expansion of steel capacity in the noncommunist world at least through 1990. The LDCs may approach the Lima Declaration figure of 25 percent of world steel output by 1990. Because LDCs account for more than 70 percent of the world's population and use relatively little steel (an average 30 kg per person per year), the potential for greater steel consumption underscores the likelihood of increases in capacity, especially for those NICs with the potential for rapid economic development.

For the immediate future, cost constraints will favor expansion of existing facilities (despite their limitations), over construction of new integrated plants. Some minimills and small electric furnace operations will be built in smaller developing countries. Diversified industrial complexes require enormous amounts of capital as well as a highly skilled labor force; these are increasingly problematic for most LDCs.

Notwithstanding the rapid growth of LDC steel consumption, LDC steel mills will wreak considerable havoc on the world steel market through the 1980s. The global steel market in the late 1980s and early 1990s probably will be characterized by.

slower growth in global consumption and production;

reduction of steel imports by NICs;

further increase in exports by NICs; and

definite slackening of exports from such older steel producers as Japan, the United States, and the EC.

Japan could be particularly hard pressed, because sales to LDCs account for about 50 percent of its steel exports. Greater sales to communist countries would not offset the decline of exports to the LDCs.

The NIC steel phenomenon is not a consequence of generalized forces of economic growth and industrialization, but of unusual circumstances and forces in a few societies at a particular time. Some LDCs will emerge as NICs, and some may even become major exporters, but the number will be limited. There is, therefore, no danger of the LDCs as a whole taking more than 25 percent of the market (in steel or other industries). Not surprisingly, several steel-producing NICs are becoming more important in such steel-intensive products as autos, hardware, cutlery, ships, and electrical and mechanical machinery parts.

The ability of NICs to increase production and take a growing share of domestic and world markets depends on a wide range of factors. In the past, high capital and startup costs have caused problems for new steelmakers. Now, however, changes in steel technology favor the NICs.

NOTES

1. A large number of sources are used in the body of this chapter. Statistical references come primarily from the series *World Steel Dynamics* (New York: Paine Webber Mitchell Hutchins, Inc.); publications of the OECD; and U.S. government publications.

2. Kenneth Warren, *World Steel: An Economic Geography* (New York: Crane Russak, 1975); and Lennart Friedan, *Instability in the International Steel Market: A Study of Import and Export Fluctuations* (Stockholm: Beckmans, 1972). These studies document the global upheaval in the steel industry.

3. The world has experienced shifts in steel production in the past. The United Kingdom controlled 37 percent of world steelmaking in 1870 but accounts for only 2.8 percent today. The United States supplied 49 percent of the world's steel in 1950 but only 12 percent by 1982. Japanese steelmaking grew from 2.5 percent of world production in 1950 to more than 16 percent by 1975. From less than 6 percent in 1960, the LDCs surpassed 11 percent in 1983.

4. William T. Hogan, "Future Steel Plants in the Third World," *Iron and Steel Engineer*, November 1977, pp.25–37, discusses these problems in more detail.

5. Credit terms for steel equipment are still covered under OECD export-credit arrangements with maximum allowable credit terms of

8 years and 12.4 percent interest for category I nations (OECD and the Soviet Union);

8–10 years and 10.7 percent interest for category II nations (NICs); and

10 years and 9.5 percent interest for category III nations (other LDCs).

APPENDIX

Forecasts of Total LDC Crude Steel Capacity to 1990 and 2000 (million metric tons)

	1990*	2000*
Latin America	61.33	73.58
Brazil	27.08	29.00
Mexico	16.26	20.80
Argentina	7.28	9.00
Venezuela	6.10	7.40
Chile	1.17	1.50
Colombia	1.07	2.00
Peru	0.87	1.20
Cuba	0.35	0.68
Others	1.15	2.00
Africa	20.07	28.72
South Africa	12.00	14.00
Nigeria	3.10	4.40
Algeria	2.06	4.06
Libya	1.32	2.50
Zimbabwe	1.00	1.50
Tunisia	0.20	0.50
Morocco	0.20	0.50
Others	0.19	1.26

APPENDIX—Continued

	1990*	2000*
Middle East	8.92	14.44
Iran	4.00	5.10
Egypt	2.69	3.00
Saudi Arabia	0.85	3.00
Iraq	0.44	1.00
Qatar	0.42	0.84
Israel	0.25	0.50
Syria	0.12	0.25
Others	0.15	0.75
Far East	117.92	148.38
China	51.00	60.00
India	22.55	30.00
South Korea	19.00	22.60
North Korea	10.00	15.00
Taiwan	8.25	10.50
Indonesia	2.05	2.50
Pakistan	1.06	1.06
Malaysia	1.00	2.00
Thailand	0.75	1.50
Singapore	0.75	1.16
Bangladesh	0.60	1.00
Philippines	0.50	0.50
Hong Kong	0.26	0.26
Others	0.15	0.30
Total LDCs	208.24	265.12
Total world	1,057.14	1,169.31

Source: World Steel Dynamics.

*Estimated.

6

Copper Prices, Consumption, and Production: An Analysis of Import Restrictions

In mid–1984 a choice of recommendations concerning refined and blister copper import measures was offered the U.S. president by members of the International Trade Commission: an annual quota of 425,000 short tons (ST); a five-cent addition to existing tariffs; or retention of the current regime. The president had to decide by September 7, 1984, what steps to take, if any, to alleviate the injury that imports were allegedly doing to domestic producers.

Using an econometric analysis of the respective impacts on U.S. producers and consumers of several different quotas or tariffs on refined and blister copper, certain scenarios became evident. First, a base-case forecast, assuming the absence of new protective measures, was provided. Next, forecasts assuming a quota with different resulting import levels were inspected. Finally, forecasts assuming tariffs at several different levels, both per pound and ad valorem were studied. An appendix lists the exogenous variables used in the copper model utilized in the forecasts, and describes some of the underlying assumptions and methodology.

EFFECT OF CONTINUING THE PRESENT REGIME UNCHANGED

Table 6.1 projects certain base-case data. According to these projections, the U.S. producer price would increase from 75 cents/lb. in 1983–1984 to 87 cents/lb. in 1985, continuing steadily upward to $1.20/lb. in 1989 (a level well short of the $1.38/lb. averaged by the London Metals Exchange [LME] copper price in April 1974). Domestic consumption and production would rise rapidly in 1985, somewhat less in 1986–87, and very little in 1988–89. Imports would pursue a zigzag pattern, reaching in 1989 about the same level as in 1983.

THE EFFECT OF A QUOTA

If a 425,000 ST quota on the import of refined and blister copper were introduced, its impact would depend heavily on how and whether the aggregate volume of copper imports and exports in ore, concentrate, and wire bar form (as well as blister and refined copper) would change.

If the current regime were continued, aggregate net imports would have reached 345,000 ST in 1984. Assuming a continuation through 1989 of this overall net import level under a 425,000 ST quota, the producer price would rise from 75 cents/lb. in 1983 to 86 cents/lb. in 1984 and $1.12/lb. in 1985, then staying roughly level until 1988 ($1.19/lb.) before jumping to $1.35/lb. in 1989. In this case, the producer price would remain more than 10 cents/lb. above the projected LME price for the next five years, and the price of scrap would almost double (44 cents to 82 cents/lb.) between 1983 and 1985. Annual U.S. consumption in 1989, at 3,550,000 ST, would be about 2 percent below the 3,615,000 ST projected under the current U.S. import regime. On the other hand, 1989 U.S. production, at 1,534,000 ST, would be almost 7 percent above the current regime projection of 1,434,000 ST.

An alternative projection under the 425,000 ST annual quota, in the absence of additional import restrictions, would allow for the diversion into the U.S. market of copper ore, concentrate, and wire bar in partial compensation for the displacement of refined and blister copper imports (see Table 6.2). In this scenario, net annual copper imports would rise to 595,000 ST. The producer price would drop to an average 56 cents/lb. in 1984, almost 20 cents/lb. lower than under the current regime, before recovering to 88 cents/lb. in 1985 (about the same as under the current regime) and then continuing to levels averaging a little less than 10 cents/lb. below the current regime projection during

Table 6.1.
United States: Copper Prices, Consumption, Production, Imports

	U.S. Producer prices (per pound)	Percent Change from previous year	U.S. consumption[a] (1000 ST)	Percent change from previous year	U.S. mine production (1000 ST)	Percent change from previous year	U.S. net imports[b] (1000 ST)	Percent change from previous year
Projection Under Current Import Regime								
1984	75¢	0.2	2,925	3.3	1,193	3.5	432	17.9
5	87	15.4	3,141	7.4	1,265	6.0	545	26
6	96	10.1	3,277	4.3	1,328	5.0	527	-3.2
7	$1.03	7.0	3,441	5.0	1,366	2.9	534	1.3
8	1.09	6.2	3,532	2.6	1,393	2.0	507	-5.1
9	1.20	10.0	3,615	2.4	1,434	2.9	511	0.7
Recorded Figures, 1979–1983								
1983	75¢	5.4	2,833	8.9	1,152	-8.2	524	166.1
82	71	-14.1	2,600	-19.0	1,256	-25.9	197	5.9
81	83	-15.9	3,211	6.8	1,695	30.2	186	-39.3
80	99	10.3	3,006	-13.4	1,301	-18.2	306	243.1
79	90	37.8	3,470	2.5	1,591	2.5	89	-73.0

Source: Data Resources Inc.

[a]Consumption of refined copper plus direct use of old and new scrap
[b]Includes refined copper, unrefined primary copper products, and scrap

Table 6.2
Effects of 425,000-ST US Quota on U.S. Producer Price, Production, and Consumption of Copper

	Price under quota (per pound)	Percent Change from base[a] price	Production under quota (1000 ST)	Percent change from base[a] prod. fig.	Consumption under quota (1000 ST)	Percent change from base[a] cons. fig.
A. Annual Net Imports, 1984–89: 345,000 ST[b]						
1984	86¢	+14	1,251	+4	2,911	0
1985	$1.12	28	1,415	+12	3,092	−2
1986	1.09	13	1,457	+10	3,209	−2
1987	1.16	13	1,480	+8	3,355	−3
1988	1.19	9	1,481	+6	3,450	−3
1989	1.35	12	1,534	+7	3,550	−3
B. Annual Net Imports, 1984–89: 595,000 ST[b]						
1984	56¢	−25	1,071	−10	2,953	−1
1985	88	+1	1,220	−4	3,170	−1
1986	90	−6	1,280	−4	3,316	−1
1987	98	−5	1,322	−3	3,489	−1
1988	96	−12	1,313	−6	3,563	−1
1989	$1.11	−7	1,360	−5	3,661	−1

Source: Data Resources, Inc.

[a]Base quantities are quantities projected under current import regime.

[b]This aggregate figure covers refined and blister copper, ore, concentrate, matte, and scrap. Case 8 assumes an increase in U.S. imports of copper except blister and refined, together with some decline in the export of refined copper and ore.

the subsequent four-year period. The producer price would also be lower than the LME price at the same (595,000 mt) import level, and the differential would increase during the period 1985–89. Between 1984 and 1989, U.S. consumption (which in 1989 would reach 3,661,000 ST) would average a little more than 1 percent over the current regime projections. However, output projected at 1,361,000 ST would be more than 4 percent lower than under the current regime, or about 20 percent above the depressed (1,142,700 ST) 1983 production level.

IMPACTS OF TARIFFS

Evidence on the impact of measures that were mentioned as alternatives to quotas on refined and blister copper imports depends on the rate of the tariff imposed. Overall, increasing the U.S. tariff on blister and refined copper would have the following effects

The domestic producer price would be higher, but the increase in price would in most cases be less than the increase in the tariff;

The LME price would be lower, but the decrease would in most cases be less than the increase in the tariff;

The difference between the producer price and the LME price would be approximately equal to the tariff plus transport costs; and

U.S. net imports of copper would decrease.

Tariffs have the same general effects as quotas, but are generally less reliable tools in controlling import quantities. The model was simulated to forecast a fixed tariff on primary copper products of 5 cents/lb., 10 cents/lb., and 15 cents/lb. and, alternatively, an ad valorem tariff of 15 percent and 25 percent.

Table 6.3 presents estimates of the changes in the domestic producers' price that would have resulted from these tariffs. The ad valorem tariffs would have resulted in much greater increases in the domestic producer price than the 5 cents/lb. or 10 cents/lb. tariffs.

Tariffs of 5 cents/lb. and 10 cents/lb. would have had minimal impact on the producer price, the price of scrap, and the LME price of copper. The producer price in the base forecast was 87

Table 6.3
Impact of Fixed and Ad Valorem Tariffs

	Producer Price	Change in Producer Price from Base Case Cents/lb.	U.S. Production	Percentage Change in U.S. Production	U.S. Consumption (ST)	Percentage Change in U.S. Consumption	Net Imports (ST)	Percentage Change in Net Import
Fixed Tariff 5 cents/lb.								
1985	91	4	1,291	2.0	3,132	0.2	511	-6.2
1986	100	4	1,358	2.2	3,262	0.4	487	-10.6
1987	107	4	1,398	2.3	3,420	0.6	488	-8.6
1988	113	4	1,426	2.3	3,510	0.6	460	-9.2
1989	124	4	1,466	2.2	3,593	0.6	465	-9.0
Fixed Tariff 10 cents/lb.								
1985	94	7	1,316	4.0	3,122	0.6	479	-12.1
1986	104	8	1,387	4.4	3,247	0.9	447	-15.1
1987	111	8	1,429	4.6	3,399	1.2	443	-17.0
1988	118	9	1,458	4.6	3,489	1.2	414	-18.3
1989	129	9	1,497	4.3	3,573	1.1	420	-17.8

Fixed Tariff 15 cents/lb.

1985	98	11	1,341	6.0	3,113	-0.8	446	-18.1
1986	107	11	1,417	6.7	3,233	-1.3	408	-22.5
1987	115	12	1,460	6.8	3,380	-1.7	398	-25.4
1988	122	12	1,489	6.8	3,469	-1.7	369	-27.2
1989	133	13	1,528	6.5	3,553	-1.7	375	-26.6

Ad Valorem Tariff of 15 percent

1985	96	9	1,328	4.9	3,118	0.7	462	-15.2
1986	107	11	1,407	5.9	3,239	-1.1	420	-20.3
1987	115	12	1,456	6.5	3,386	-1.5	406	-23.9
1988	123	13	1,491	7.0	3,471	-1.7	368	-27.4
1989	135	15	1,537	7.1	3,551	-1.7	365	-28.5

Ad Valorem Tariff of 25 Percent

1985	102	15	1,368	8.1	3,104	-1.1	410	-24.7
1986	114	18	1,458	9.7	3,216	-1.8	352	-33.2
1987	123	20	1,515	10.9	3,353	-2.5	324	-39.3
1988	132	23	1,554	11.5	3,435	-2.7	280	-44.7
1989	145	25	1,603	11.7	3,512	-2.8	272	-46.7

Source: Data Resources, Inc.

cents/lb. in 1985 and $1.20/lb. in 1989. A 5 cents/lb. tariff would have made the price 91 cents/lb. in 1985 and $1.24/lb. by 1989, while a 10 cents/lb. tariff would have made the price 94 cents/lb. in 1985 and $1.29/lb. in 1989. Neither U.S. production nor consumption would have been greatly affected under these tariff scenarios. At 15 cents/lb. in 1989, the price would move to 98 cents/lb. by 1985 and $1.33/lb. in 1989, with a robust increase in U.S. production and a drop in consumption. Ad valorem tariffs would have had similar effects, with a 15 percent ad valorem bringing prices to 96 cents/lb. by 1985 and $1.35/lb. in 1989; and a 25 percent ad valorem, $1.02/lb. in 1985 and $1.45/lb. in 1989.

CONCLUSIONS

The major conclusions of an econometric analysis of this sort suggest that:

1. U.S. consumers would pay heavily if a 425,000 ST annual quota during the period 1984–89 resulted in the maintenance of current aggregate net annual copper import levels (blister, refined ore, concentrate, and wire bar). U.S. consumers would profit, however, if aggregate net import levels rise in accordance with the other proposed scenario. Foreign consumers of blister and refined copper in the world market including fabricators—would experience lower costs if U.S. aggregate net import levels remain the same, but would experience higher costs if U.S. aggregate net import levels rise above 595,000 ST.

2. A quota on refined or blister copper imports could be partly circumvented by imports of ore, concentrate, and wire bar.

3. Copper prices would be considerably higher during the late 1980s even without the restrictive measures of quotas or tariffs.

4. The effects of 5 cents/lb. or 10 cents/lb. fixed tariffs word prove minimal, while a 15 cent/lb. tariff, and ad valorem tariffs of 15 and 25 percent respectively, would have greater impact on both prices and U.S. copper production.

The President decided not to impose any new restrictions on the import of copper into the United States. His decision, a hallmark in the trade policy of his administration, was hailed by

free-trade proponents and condemned by protectionists. Ana-
lyzing the forecasts of various protective measures provides one
set of econometric reasons why he was so inclined.

APPENDIX

The McNicol copper model links copper demand, supply, and prices
in the United States and several major exporters and importers of
copper in a simultaneous econometric model consisting of 27 behavioral
equations, 38 exogenous variables and 9 identities. Projected exogenous
variables provide various forecasts. The structure of the model is built
around the following accounting identity, which equates demand and
supply:

(1) $Qj + Ij = QMj + QS = NMj + SDj$

where, Qj = copper consumption
ΔIj = change in end-of-period copper stocks
QMj = mine production
QSj = recovery of scrap
NMj = region's net imports (excluding semi-fabricated
products)
SDj = statistical discrepancy (exogenous)

Copper consumption in the United States is a function of the current
and lagged prices of copper, the price of aluminum (exogenous to the
model and forecast by the Data Resources, Inc. [DRI] U.S. Aluminum
Model), and industrial production in the United States (exogenous to
the model and held constant at 3 percent a year for this simulation).
Mine production is a function of the price of copper, the index of mining
costs in the United States (exogenous), and refinery capacity (exogenous). Recovery of copper from scrap is a function of the reservoir of
semifabricated copper products in the United States, the price of copper
scrap, average weekly earnings of production workers in copper semi-
fabricating industries (exogenous), and the index of wages in semifab-
ricating industries (exogenous). Net imports are determined as a
residual from the identity of equation (1), above. The main variable
linking the two blocks of the model, the United States and the rest of the
world (ROW), is the price of copper on the LME. This price is determined in the ROW block of the model for other market economies, and
has significant influence on the block for the United States. It is the main
path by which events external to the United States affect copper demand, supply, and prices in the United States.

Exogenous variables utilized in this copper model include

Index of U.S. durable manufacturing
Index of principal mining expenses
1970 base of U.S. weekly earnings
Average weekly earnings of U.S. copper workers
Average weekly earnings of U.S. copper miners
Refining capacity
Change in durable goods inventory
Copper stocks (dummy variable)
U.S. government stocks of copper
U.S. supply discrepancy*
Price of U.S. aluminum
Producer price index of U.S. durable manufacturing
Mine capacity
  Canada
  Chile
  Peru
  Zaire
  Zambia
  Rest of World
Industrial production index
  Canada
  Europe
  Japan
  Other Buyers
Index of mining exports, Japan
Index of mining exports, Zambia
Index of wages, Japan
Consumer price index for Europe
Price of aluminum, West Germany

*The estimates were reduced by entering positive values for the exogenous variables called "statistical discrepancies." Sizable unreported inventories of copper are known to exist and the data base of the model is such that withdrawals from the stocks would appear in the statistical discrepancies. The values for the statistical discrepancies were set to trend down from recent historical values to the historical average of 50,000 ST per year.

Consumption of copper, other exporters
Net imports of copper, western countries
Supply discrepancy, outside United States*
Strikes (dummy variable)
New entrants (dummy variable)
Two-price system (dummy variable)

7

Bauxite-Aluminum: Changing Production, Jamaica, and National Security

Aluminum, which comes from processed alumina derived from bauxite, is the most abundant nonferrous metal and the third most abundant element on the earth's surface, being exceeded in amount only by oxygen and silicon. About 8 percent by weight of the earth's crust is composed of bauxite.[1] Although aluminum is so abundant it is produced commercially almost entirely from bauxite. Large deposits of the mineral are found in many parts of the world, but mostly in tropical or subtropical areas far from the big aluminum markets.[2]

The term "bauxite" was first introduced by Berthier in 1821 for sediments rich in alumina from the vicinity of Les Baux, in the Alpilles region of France. The term has since been used for weathering products rich in alumina but low in alkalis, alkaline, earths, and silica. The term "bauxite ore" applies to bauxites that are economically mineable at present or in the foreseeable future, containing not less than 45 percent $A1_2O_3$ and not more than 20 percent Fe_2O_3, and 3–5 percent combined silica.[3]

Aluminum, the now popular nonfuel metal obtained from bauxite, made its public debut in 1893, as the statue of Eros in Piccadilly Circus, London.[4] Its widespread application in fields experiencing economic growth—high speed travel, electrical industries, building, mass consumption goods, transport and storage of chemicals, tourism and leisure, and defense indus-

An earlier version of this chapter was written with assistance from the Center for Economics and National Security.

tries—quickly secured for aluminum a prominent place in advanced industrial economies.

The most versatile of all metals because of its lightness, structural strength and durability, aluminum has been given a preeminent place in construction of faster vehicles—spacecraft, jets, trains, and small car engines. Its evenness and speed of distributing heat or cold make it especially useful for appliances, utensils, and foil. Efficient conductivity explains why it is drawn into wire for high-tension power lines. Anticorrosive nontoxic properties endow it with unassailable advantages in containers for chemicals and cans for drinks. Superb alloying qualities make aluminum highly adaptable in multitudes of industrial uses. Such merits are further augmented by its attractiveness. We in the United States have come to depend on aluminum for many purposes, including those of national economic and security purposes.

In world wars and other previous conflicts the provision of adequate supplies of basic materials was the prime objective of national policy. In the past we have found ourselves "unprepared without plans for economic mobilization."[5] What are the prospects for supply disruptions and possible cutoff of bauxite-aluminum now so vital to the industrial base of the United States and the North Atlantic Treaty Organization (NATO)? What are the implications for national security? How would various sectors in the economy be affected by actions such as these? What can be done to overcome our vulnerability?

Answering these questions demands careful analysis of the bauxite-aluminum industry itself, beginning with the mining and processing of bauxite. We need to understand and document the unstable market and politically sensitive countries of present resource wealth. These raw-materials problems call for assessment of political risk, economic calculation of present capacity and demand, and strategic study of present supply security. The case of Jamaica offers some unique and realistic insights into the larger bauxite-aluminum picture.

Along with the concern over reliability and vulnerability of supplies, which requires a diffusion study of the sectors of the U.S. economy affected, the possibility of a deliberate Soviet policy to worsen the U.S. and NATO materials position—either by becoming a world trade power in minerals as its own resources begin to become depleted, or by planning mischief in the Caribbean Basin or other vital sealanes where items such as bauxite and alumina are transported.

While alerting ourselves to the problems listed above, we must also suggest remedies and inspect the options of an updated program of material stockpiles, a more aggressive approach to materials substitution and conservation that would include government and private-market actors, the better to insure against severe losses or national calamity caused by massive interruptions. Various initiatives will be evaluated including the role of the U.S. Federal Emergency Management Agency (FEMA), U.S. foreign policy, and the encouragement of the private sector in developing countries with bauxite deposits.

BAUXITE AND ALUMINUM: MINING AND PROCESSING

The international bauxite-aluminum industry has been characterized as an international oligopoly with potential for cartel-like behavior being undertaken both by the firms and certain countries which produce bauxite. The International Bauxite Association (IBA) is the counterpart to OPEC.[6]

The aluminum industry consists of five stages of production: bauxite, aluminum, primary aluminum, ingot, fabricated aluminum products and end products containing aluminum. In stages one through three a small number of multinational corporations (MNCs) have become vertically integrated and exercise considerable control. Of the six major international companies, four are North American firms, and all six have smelting operations in North America, either wholly owned or through partnerships; 63 percent of world smelting capacity is controlled by Alcan Ltd., Alcoa, Reynolds, Kaiser, Pechiney and Swiss Aluminum A.G. There is no free market for bauxite or alumina. In stage four the same large companies are involved but, in addition, a number of individual fabricators and suppliers of scrap metal compete. A market does exist and prices of ingot are published.

World bauxite production involves 26 countries producing 86 million tons of bauxite in recent years, a decrease of 3 percent from 1980. Australia, Jamaica, Guinea, and Brazil accounted for 64 percent of world production. World alumina production from 26 countries totaled 32.3 million tons, down 3 percent from 1980. Australian and U.S. refineries produced 40 percent of the total.

Domestic U.S. production of bauxite is small, and recent alumina production, at nine Bayer-process refineries, measured 5.96 million tons, 12 percent below 1980 production.[7] U.S. bauxite reserves, 90 percent of which come from Arkansas, would only provide 11 percent of U.S. consumption if they were relied on completely. It is estimated that these mines could if pressed supply at most four to five years worth of domestic consumption before being totally exhausted. U.S. bauxite however is very costly to mine, due to location, field size, stripping ratio, and high silica content.[8] Consumption of foreign aluminum in the United States by contrast is minimal, but aluminum is increasingly becoming a primary U.S. export.

The United States has become increasingly reliant on imported aluminum-derived materials. The proportion of total metal demand met by old scrap is only about 10 percent. As the world's leading consumer of aluminum, whose sources lie outside this country, the United States finds itself in a potentially dangerous position. U.S. share of world aluminum stands at 33 percent, with the Soviet Union, Japan, West Germany, France, Italy, and the United Kingdom the next largest consumers, in descending order.[9]

UNSTABLE MARKETS

The world's base metal producers are beginning to see a recovery from the worst years since the 1930s.[10] But more than a few companies have shut down mines and abandoned new projects, even half-completed ones, because of the recent slump.[11] Chase Econometrics predicted a 1.5 percent growth per year after 1981 for the container industry, 3.5 percent in construction, and 2.8 percent in transportation.[12] S.R. Spector, in a United Nations International Development Organization (UNIDO) paper, also forecast a real metal shortage, according to demand projections, after 1982. The potential difficulties in supply are due to strikes, production problems, energy shortages, and not necessarily mineral supply.[13] An Organization for Economic Cooperation and Development (OECD) report, on the other hand, saw some margin of excess capacity without the erosion of prices, increased government support for investments, and perhaps, structured and cyclical changes in demand, so long as promotion is left entirely to the industries.[14]

In the past few years the aluminum industry has been so badly hurt by overcapacity and aggressive pricing that domestic producers chose to hold back expansion, run at near capacity, and raise prices as far as demand and the law would allow. *Business Week* argued that the "long-run outlook for domestic supply is less than favorable for aluminum users," pointing to Alcoa, which has been unwilling to build new plants to supply Detroit unless a long-term commitment from autoworkers to take specific amounts of output is secured in advance.[15] Overall the chief beneficiary seems to be Alcan Aluminum, Ltd. The Canadian company has now captured 70 percent of U.S. aluminum imports. The increasing internationalization of processing and fabrication is in line with aluminum producers' quest for profitability. The consequences of this gradual decline of the U.S. industry, however, leave both Detroit and U.S. defense planners in doubt. It is wise to recall that the United States has experienced aluminum shortages in 1950–53, 1966, 1972–74, and 1975–77.

It is also worth noting that availability, price of energy, and changes in electric power drastically affect the aluminum industry. Depletion of bauxite may be nearly impossible, as it is plentiful and widespread, but the need and cost of increased hydroelectric power and coal-based energy to produce aluminum could make the future outlook problematic.[16] When we take into account the comparatively few mineable bauxite deposits of high quality, problems of economy of scale, state interest, capital intensity, and the need for electric power, we cannot be as certain of supplies as might otherwise be the case. Of particular importance is the location of smelters in other countries less plagued by the question of electricity, safety, and environmental regulation. There is a noticeable tendency developing in response to desires of producing countries to locate alumina-processing facilities near bauxite deposits, thereby reducing transportation costs. This "streaming down" has obvious ramifications for security and reliability of supply.[17]

In actuality, however, each major firm uses bauxite from a number of different sources, thus reducing risk of interruptions of supply all at once. The many joint ventures with foreign governments that have evolved over the past ten years also lessen the chance of total supply disruption. Taking the historical view, capacity in aluminum growth has nearly outrun demand. After the Korean War, 1950s capacity grew 8 percent per annum. In the decade before the oil crisis, 9.2 percent; in the 1970s, only 2 percent was added each year.[18] The 1980s have been nearly stagnant. According to *Multinational Business*,

The political pressures upon energy supply have been matched in recent years by the well-publicized political pressure from the raw material suppliers. In practice few companies smelt primary aluminum, which means that it is very difficult for bauxite suppliers to impose unilaterally prices unacceptable to the whole industry.[19]

Recent forecasts show a rise of under 4 percent a year in aluminum production into the foreseeable future. However, since 1978 the United States has been a net importer of aluminum. It seems that MNCs are content to see imports take a greater share of the U.S. market, and are themselves investing heavily in Australia and Brazil. With 54 percent of all beverage cans made of aluminum, U.S. cars using 14 pounds more of the metal since 1978—up to over 128 pounds per car, and with government regulations mandating yet lighter cars for fuel efficiency, as well as demonstrable strategic defense needs, the internationalization of the industry can be questioned from a national security point of view.

W. Malenbaum, in *World Demand for Raw Materials in 1985*, forecasts the world demand for raw materials using an intensity of use (I-U) method whereby

$$I - U = iDt - GDPt$$

(iDt = demand for mineral i in time t and GDPt = Gross Domestic Product in time t)[20].

If I-U is plotted against GDP per capita for aluminum, then the relationship is positive but the increase is at a decreasing rate. Thus, with increased income as measured by GDP per capita, the intensity of use of aluminum increases at a decreasing rate. The study shows aluminum as the only raw material for which this relationship holds. The favorable position of aluminum is attributed to the widening scope for further displacement by aluminum of other metals. If this occurs, which seems less than certain, an even more jeopardized state results, and competition for the metal could ensue.

In summary, both aluminum capacity and demand are growing, and can expect slow growth, but these needs will not necessarily be met in the United States. The aluminum industry rode out the recessionary years and recovered, relocating overseas because of certain supplies, cheap energy and lower production and labor costs. Both bauxite and aluminum supplies can be expected to experience further shifts and economic cycles with slackened demand.[21] If demand should pick up or dramatically increase, however, there will be both a time lag in supply availability and an uncompetitive price structure due to irregular and excess demand. The results of this scenario on U.S. industries, and particularly defense industries, should be considered.

Another fear that has materialized in the bauxite-aluminum industry is cartelization. Although the producing countries are unlikely to organize a major OPEC-like mechanism there is motivation behind the International Bauxite Association (IBA). Hoping to improve terms of trade, capture larger portions of rising economic rents, conserve limited resources, and assure a base for the development of domestic processing industries, the bauxite-producing countries founded their cartel in 1974. The overall effectiveness of the IBA depends on numerous factors including control of export markets, production and reserves, the ability to forego export earnings and remain immune to retaliation, and the sharing of strongly held and cohesive economic and political objectives. Needless to say, the mineral must also be in demand, with relatively unresponsive price changes for which substitution or alternative products are not too readily available.[22]

The IBA has not demonstrated much clout but because the

capital costs of new capacity are so high, a cartel in bauxite-aluminum does have at least the potential for success. New aluminum smelters in the United States in the mid–60s, when many new facilities with plants and fabrication abilities came on line, cost about $1,000 per annual ton of reduction capacity. Today a replica, with no new technology except effluent controls, costs more than $2,500 per annum a ton.[23] This includes the estimated costs to industry due to pollution controls of approximately $0.025 per pound or $100 million per year.[24]

When the IBA was formed, bauxite taxes levied by Jamaica and other countries were increased from $1.50 per ton to $15.00 and then to $18.00, causing delivered U.S. costs approximately to double. Since 1978 the IBA has tied members' prices to American Metal Market quotations for aluminum ingot, or about $24.00 per metric ton. Virtually all U.S. bauxite and alumina imported into the United States comes from IBA members; 100 percent of Canadian supply is IBA produced. These members account for 80 percent of noncommunist production and 68 percent of world reserves. Brazil and Cameroons, major non-IBA reserve holders, with 37 and 11 years, respectively, of world supply at 1976 consumption rates, must also be considered. Noncommunist world supply shares stand at: Australia 29 percent, Jamaica 22 percent, Surinam 10 percent, Guinea 9 percent, and Guyana 4 percent; while U.S. import shares as a percent of the market are: Jamaica 40 percent, Australia 25 percent, Surinam 16 percent, Guinea 5 percent, and Guyana 5 percent.

Overall it seems, even with cartelization, that a damaging cutoff of bauxite is most unlikely. Export embargoes even by key producers would be costly to the United States but in the long run would be adjusted toward other supply sources. The argument could be made, however, that the high costs associated with a cutoff justify the maintenance of contingency stockpiles. According to a Charles River Associates research report, "the possibility of short-run monopoly behavior is important since alumina plants are specialized to use particular types of bauxite; this limitation gives individual countries, such as Jamaica, great short-run power which would damage the U.S."[25] The locational advantage and the high dependency on bauxite for national income of the Caribbean producers, where large foreign exchange is earned and government revenues enhanced, means that even short-term monopoly actions are not in the best interest of those countries. The principal issue remains longer-term IBA pricing, although preparedness for worse-case scenarios is advisable.

As a percentage, the United States is more dependent on IBA bauxite producers than for energy from OPEC countries. Bauxite, the sixth largest item in world trade, has, however, a demand curve with significant elasticity. Increases in cost only induce the use of copper, plastics, steel, and other materials. Since "the present tax level for most bauxite is about 12 percent of cost of refined aluminum; excluding IBA taxes the cost drops to 6 percent. Thus only very large increases in price would cause noticeable decreases in the total demand for aluminum."[26] This means that the United States is in a good bargaining position vis-à-vis bauxite producers. The use of non-IBA bauxite, establishment of tariffs, diplomatic pressures and trade incentives, preferences, and concessions make a long-term embargo very improbable. Australia is particularly unlikely to participate in an IBA embargo against the United States, its strongest military ally.

Charles River Associates puts overall price elasticity of demand at 0.15 short range (SR) and 0.7 long range (LR) and states these moderate figures "indicate that there are substantial advantages to users from using aluminum rather than substitutes. A shortfall in aluminum could have major dislocation effects on using markets, as could major increases in the price of aluminum."[27] Although the probability of loss is not large, Woods and Burrows, in *The World Aluminum-Bauxite Market*, by use of an econometric model show that total loss due to an IBA embargo would be $.042 billion at one year; $1.73 billion at two years; $3.72 billion after three years; and $4.27 billion extended to four years' duration; these figures assume stockpiles, without which the costs incurred could be twice as great.[28]

POLITICAL RISKS

Bauxite supply is affected by natural developments, so assessment of political risk by producing countries is in order. Country risk analysis looks at exposure to a loss in cross-border lending or investing, caused by events in a particular country that are at least to some extent under the control of the government, but definitely not under the control of a private enterprise or individual. Political risk can be equated with political change and instability, as well as other forms of intervention including civil war and revolution, extremist takeovers, war, occupation, riots, disorder, strikes, or corruption. These problems often result in destruction, nationalization, or indigenization of assets.

As noted, bauxite suppliers are numerous, and Australia, a low-risk country, has the greatest reported resources of any single country. Guinea, a higher risk country, has witnessed expansion of its bauxite production while both Guyana and Surinam, high-risk Caribbean producers, are slowed by limitations on total resources and serious political problems. By 2000, Brazil, a low political risk country even in its present economic state, will be the fourth largest producer of bauxite through joint measures with foreign aluminum companies. However, Brazil's strategy is intended to offset other nonferrous metal imports and is therefore of domestic, not export, significance.

Jamaica has large bauxite production in close proximity to the United States. However, alienation of investors in the 1970s and political turmoil have made Jamaica a question in the minds of many industry analysts. For this reason it is worthwhile to look at Jamaica as a microcosm or case study of bauxite-aluminum suppliers. Much can be gleaned from a detailed study of the Jamaican situation.

JAMAICA: A CASE STUDY IN RISK ASSESSMENT

One way to view the political and economic risks is to focus microscopically and to analyze the structure, production and market characteristics of the Jamaican bauxite industry and their relationship to the Jamaican domestic governmental policies formulated in the period from 1972–82.

Five North American–based companies along with the government of Jamaica totally control Jamaican bauxite and aluminum production.[29] We need to attempt to understand the strategies of these MNCs in order fully to document their impact on the development of Jamaica, and to ascertain the likelihood of supply disruptions to the United States.

On November 24, 1981, President Reagan directed the FEMA to acquire close to 1.6 million tons of Jamaican trade bauxite.[30] This acquisition was considered a national security issue and was initiated and implemented in line with a responsible program for procuring basic raw materials vital to the U.S. defense program. What was behind the purchase of Jamaican bauxite? And why did it come at that point in time?

Bauxite is the only mineral used in the production of aluminum, a major element to the industrial base of the United States. In addition, bauxite remains a vital raw material in the production of the U.S. military buildup. In order to decrease the nation's military vulnerability, this acquisition program was seen as a necessary first step. Stockpiling the mineral from which aluminum is made gives the United States a more secure supply of this important strategic item.

The effects of the MNCs' involvement in and U.S. dependence on Jamaican bauxite production is an area that must be explored. It seems that certain factors affecting the performance of the industry lie outside of Jamaica, influencing both the expansion and production of bauxite, and also the very development of Jamaica.[31] Jamaican domestic governmental policies formulated in this atmosphere should be seen as considerably influenced by pertinent outside factors and longstanding domestic political conflicts and ideologies in a Third World setting. By examining the structures that affect increased participation by Jamaica in the processing and marketing of bauxite, alumina, and aluminum, further insight can be gained not only into the extent to which these outside forces have influenced the formulation of policies in Jamaica, but whether or not the development and procurement(?) of minerals such as Jamaican bauxite leads to a relationship of interdependence between industrial and developing nations. Jamaica is as dependent on the United States for bauxite and alumina purchases as the United States is vulnerable to Jamaica for high-quality, secure supplies of the mineral.

By viewing the background and present status of the bauxite-alumina industry and looking at the political and social factors intertwined with it, we can see how the present system could be improved to each country's advantage, and most certainly to strengthen the vital national security of the United States.

Bauxite in Jamaica

Jamaican bauxite is a claylike substance consisting of a mixture of hydrated aluminum oxides and other mineral matter from which alumina (aluminum oxide) can be extracted.[32] Although technically not considered a mineral in itself, the term "bauxite" is generally used to describe the mixture in which the combination of minerals is likely to be distinguished.

Primarily the result of aluminum-bearing silicate rocks or clay-bearing limestone, bauxite is normally found under tropical conditions of contrasting wet and dry seasons. Deposits of bauxite are located in areas throughout the world including such countries as the United States, France, Greece, Jamaica, Guyana, the Soviet Union, India, and Australia.

Bauxite is by far the most important and most abundant mineral in the Caribbean island of Jamaica. It exists as a blanket with pocketlike deposits virtually covering the surface of the north to south region of the middle of the island. The largest deposits are in the parishes of St. Ann, Manchester, St. Elizabeth, and Trelawny, with smaller deposits at Clarendon and St. Catherine.[33] Ore tends to be located in the highlands approximately 1,200 feet above sea level and is located in the pockets and bowls of lime which form two-thirds of the island's bedrock. Proven current reserves are estimated to be in excess of 2,000 million metric tons.[34]

History of Jamaican Mineral Development

The presence of bauxite in Jamaica can be traced to 1869, but it was not until World War II, with the increased demand for aluminum used in military factories, that any attention was paid to the vast deposits of the mineral outside the United States and Europe. During this period tests were conducted on various soils, showing the composition of minerals. The Jamaican bauxite when analyzed was found to be unlike the ores of North

America or even Guyana, as it contained a much lower content of aluminum. Six tons of Jamaican bauxite were needed for one ton of aluminum, as opposed to only four tons of Guyana bauxite needed for the same ton.[35] This disadvantage, however, was more than compensated for by three factors favorable to bauxite production. First, Jamaican reserves were enormous and easily accessible. Second, the rock lay on the surface of the land and was easily worked. Third, the deposits were only 900 miles from the U.S. Gulf Coast ports, and transport costs were low.[36]

In contribution to the war effort, on November 26, 1942, the governor of Jamaica issued Defense Regulation No. 21, which authorized the commissioner of lands to take possession of any Jamaican bauxite as Crown property.[37] However, Jamaican bauxite was not used extensively during the Second World War, and as soon as the Jamaican government realized that their bauxite deposits would play little part in the war efforts, defense stipulations declared that government possession of bauxite property was no longer necessary.[38] Knowledge of the extent of the mineral deposits, however, soon brought three North American companies—Aluminum Limited of Montreal, Reynolds Metals Company of Virginia, and Kaiser Aluminum and Chemical Corporation of California—to Jamaica in an effort to acquire land and establish mining operations.

Aluminum demand dropped drastically at the close of World War II and was not revived until the development of the Economic Cooperation Administration (ECA) in the late 1940s and the onslaught of the Korean War.[39] The ECA was concerned with building up the U.S. stockpile of minerals that had been depleted following the Second World War. This put pressure on the two U.S. corporations, Kaiser and Reynolds, to increase their Jamaican bauxite production.

By June 5, 1952, Reynolds had begun exporting bauxite from Ocho Rios, and Kaiser followed a year later, exporting from a Jamaican south coast port. Aluminum Limited, also known as Alcan, started operations around the same time, building a processing plant near its mines in Kirkvine, Manchester, and began shipping alumina to the United States and Canada in early 1953.[40] With these steps the Jamaican bauxite industry was under way. The structure of production was in place and has remained through periods of economic expansion, recession and political turmoil.

Market Orientation to Bauxite

Alumina experienced an increased demand during the 1960s and 1970s due to an ever-expanding market for alumina and aluminum products. While most bauxite is refined into metal-grade aluminum, a growing amount was diverted into the manufacture of certain alumina chemicals. Used as an ingredient in various products, alumina was demonstrated, among other things, to make toothpaste polish teeth whiter, glass clearer, paper whiter, rubber stronger, abrasive wheels cut faster and refractories withstand higher temperatures.[41]

In other areas of the market, due to the high cost of shipping and the light weight of aluminum, aluminum products also found increased demand. One prime example was the beverage production market. From 1961, when aluminum's penetration in the metal beverage can market stood at less than 1 percent, until 1980, when market penetration was at 75 percent, the growth of the aluminum can industry was indeed phenomenal.[42]

Projected figures for the date 1980s moreover, show the aluminum can capturing 92 percent of the U.S. beverage can market.[43] Not only was this market conversion due to aluminum's light weight, but as aluminum gained an increasing market share, other factors became apparent. Consumer preference for the aluminum can was one of the major reasons for the success of the metal. It contained no lead, chilled easily, and added no after-taste. Corporations also discovered that aluminum provided an ideal printing surface for proper identification, further adding to its success.[44] In recent years many other uses for aluminum have also become apparent. Today everything from jet engines to trashcans contains some aluminum.

Production Process

There are numerous steps in the conversion of raw Jamaican bauxite into final aluminum products. These steps are: (1) bauxite mining, (2) alumina processing, (3) primary aluminum ingot, (4) fabricated aluminum products, and (5) end products containing aluminum.[45]

Only the first three of these levels are completed in Jamaica. The first stage involves the mining, crushing, washing and calcining of crude bauxite near the Jamaican site of the deposit. Bauxite, the ore of alumina, contains many impurities which must be separated from it.

At the second stage—the production of alumina—a chemical process is performed in which bauxite is mixed with a solution of caustic soda and heated in high-pressure containers to dissolve the alumina. The impurities that do not dissolve are then separated through steps of settling and filtering and, finally emerge as a "red mud." The alumina is then removed from the solution through a process known as "seeding" in which the final result is a crystallike material known as "hydrated alumina." After washing, this material is then heated to drive off excess moisture and produce alumina.[46] The third stage involves the production of aluminum ingot. At this stage smelting is used in the conversion of alumina into metal. Alumina is not smelted into aluminum in Jamaica because such a step requires a massive energy supply; hence smelters have usually been located in countries with low-cost hydroelectric power, or large supplies of coal or natural gas. Jamaica obtains almost all of its energy from imported petroleum. Therefore, smelting would be expensive, if not prohibitively so. Furthermore, smelters tend to be located in developed countries due to their large market for aluminum products.[47]

The Role of the MNC in Jamaica

From its initial production in 1952, bauxite has continued with tourism, certain export crops, and "ganga" to be one of the major, if not the foremost contributor to the Jamaican economy. Under very little governmental supervision, the bauxite-alumina industry expanded rapidly, virtually unchecked in its revenue earnings until the Manley government's Production Levy Act of 1974.

Although Jamaica was mining 14 million tons of raw bauxite a year in the early 1970s, and producing some 2.5 million tons of alumina, total revenues to the Jamaican government were $25 million per annum, allegedly showing what the democratic socialist regime called a great disparity between the revenues earned by the corporations themselves and the revenues received by the Jamaican government.[48]

With the imposition of the 1974 levy, production of total bauxite dropped from over 15 million tons in 1974 to just over 11 million tons the following year, and took an even further plunge to approximately 10 million tons in 1976.[49] Part of this reduction was due to the closure of the Revere Corporation as a result of the levy, and part was due to the remaining four corporations' partial withdrawal from production. The MNCs reasoned that their withdrawal was justified by the large inventories that had been built up by producers and consumers in 1974.[50]

Aluminum production did not pick up again until 1980 following a revising of the Bauxite Production Levy. World demand for aluminum increased so much that inventory levels noticeably declined. Of the four companies having major interests in Jamaica, the output of aluminum was up in all cases except that of Reynolds during this period.[51] In 1980 there was also an increase of 15.5 percent in alumina production, while bauxite exports continued to decline, reflecting the replacement of Jamaican ore in Kaiser and Reynolds operations with bauxite from Guinea and Brazil.[52]

The Individual MNCs in Jamaica

Alcoa

The Aluminum Company of America (Alcoa) is the world's leading producer of aluminum products. Founded in the late nineteenth century, the company and its affiliates today operate 49 plants in 15 countries and maintain 113 sales offices in cities throughout the world.[53] The company has 46,000 employees, 31,000 shareholders, and nearly $5.5 billion in assets.[54]

Alcoa's chief sources of bauxite ore are Australia, the Dominican Republic, Guinea, Jamaica, Surinam, and the United States.

JAMALCO is a joint venture association between Alcoa Minerals and Jamaica Bauxite Ltd., a company wholly owned by the government of Jamaica, established as of January 1, 1980.[55] Jamaica Bauxite Mining, Ltd., owns a 6 percent interest in JAMALCO's mining and refining assets; Alcoa controls 94 percent. Each partner receives a share of alumina production equal to its percentage interest. The management and control of JAMALCO is the responsibility of Alcoa Minerals of Jamaica.[56]

In 1979 Alcoa had an extraordinary year in Jamaica, with net income rising 61.4 percent over 1978. Net income in 1980 fell 6.9 percent on higher total revenues, while the average realized price for ingot rose 20.3 percent.[57]

Alcan

Alcan aluminum, the second largest aluminum company located in Jamaica, is a Canadian company engaged in all phases of aluminum production. Alcan operates mines in Jamaica, Malaysia, France, Brazil, India, Australia, and Guinea.[58]

In Jamaica, Alcan operates in partnership with the Jamaican government. This venture, known as JAMALCAN, came into existence on November 1, 1979, when the government acquired 7 percent of Alcan's integrated mining and refining assets, while Alcan retained ownership of 93 percent of the assets.[59]

JAMALCAN's primary production reached a record high in 1980. Inventory levels increased by 18.3 percent.[60] JAMALCAN, normally selling a higher proportion of primary as opposed to semifabricated and fabricated metal than the others, and also having a higher dependence on international markets, benefited substantially from the increased demand in European and Japanese markets.[61]

Kaiser

Kaiser is the fifth largest aluminum producer in the world, and the third largest producer in the United States. Of the major aluminum producers, Kaiser is probably the most diversified, with interests in agricultural and industrial chemicals, strontium, real estate, shipping, international commodity trading and refractories material.[62]

Kaiser Bauxite Company of Jamaica is the parent company's oldest and largest source of bauxite. As of February 1, 1980, in an agreement with the government of Jamaica, the company's name was changed to Kaiser Jamaica Bauxite Company.

Shipments declined slightly in 1980 from the previous year, yet primary ingot shipments increased significantly as a proportion of the whole.[63]

Reynolds

Reynolds is the third largest aluminum producer in North America, and until recently was the third largest in the world. Founded in 1928, Reynolds's home location is Richmond, Virginia. Reynolds has assets exceeding $3 billion, approximately 37,000 employees, 29,000 stockholders and more than 50 domestic operating locations.[64]

In September 1950, Reynolds became the first bauxite producer to be officially recognized in Jamaica. Reynolds has always played an important role in Jamaican bauxite production, yet recently it focused less of its attention on Jamaican bauxite mines, and is presently investing more in its operations in Guinea.

ALPART

In 1966 Alumina Partners of Jamaica (ALPART) was formed as a consortium of Reynolds Jamaica Alumina Ltd. (36.54 percent), Kaiser Jamaica Corp. (36.54 percent) and Anaconda Jamaica Inc. (26.92 percent).[65] Both Kaiser and Reynolds contributed bauxite deposits in St. Elizabeth and Manchester to the consortium. Kaiser also contributed its Port Kaiser shipping, bauxite-drying facilities, and rail facilities. Kaiser is the managing partner and supervisor of ALPART.[66]

The Jamaican Government and Proven Bauxite Resources

Until 1974, the role of the Jamaican government in bauxite-alumina production was minimal. Although the mineral was technically controlled by the state before the industry grew to prominence, the corporations exploiting bauxite were wholly owned subsidiaries of North American–based aluminum companies. The result was that despite Jamaica's importance in world bauxite-alumina production, the government revenue brought in by this industry was a fraction of its value.

The elections of February 1972 had a great impact on the Jamaican economic situation. With the advent of the People's National Party (PNP) government under the leadership of Michael Manley, the winds of change were evident. Coming into a country wracked by high unemployment, malnutrition, deplorable social conditions, and little revenue, Manley was also faced with a rapid increase in world inflation. The PNP's social programs started at the beginning of his first term suffered severe setbacks as worldwide inflation increased. They were also afflicted with poorly administered, if not greedy government-party controlled bureaucracies.

In 1974, in answer to the economic chaos at hand, the Jamaican government took two major steps to restore stability to the country. In February, at a conference at Conakry, Guinea, the IBA was formed; its purpose was the bringing together of major bauxite-producing countries with a "general intention to work towards the greatest possible national control and ownership of bauxite industry in each of the members territory."[67]

After forming the cartel, the socialist government of Jamaica felt better prepared to address the multinational corporations in its own bauxite-alumina industry. The Jamaican negotiating team wanted a substantial increase in government revenues from the bauxite operations, Jamaican ownership of all bauxite lands, and at least 51 percent of each company's operations on the island. The MNCs refused, and the Jamaican Parliament voted a levy on bauxite mined for export and for local processing into aluminum. They also indexed the price of the levy to the price of aluminum ingot sold in the United States, thus bypassing transfer pricing.

What developed from the controversial Bauxite Production Levy Act of 1974, the first piece of legislation indicating the new policy, was a bargaining process that took a long time to settle. This policy clearly had twin objectives: to increase government revenues from aluminum companies, and for the government itself to become a shareholder in the bauxite-alumina companies.[68] The first move was in keeping with the PNP's desire to control and benefit from the "commanding heights of the economy," and the second move in line with its view of "Jamaicanization" of the industry. The net effect of this new policy would not only increase the Jamaican government's revenue from $25 million per annum to $200 million, but would also enable it to have considerable influence over the rate at which deposits were depleted.[69]

These steps led to the threat of various U.S. reprisals, which soon filtered throughout Jamaica. Revere closed its plant because the levy had made operations economically unfeasible. For those corporations that remained, the government of Jamaica began purchasing share in local operations.

By 1981 Jamaica owned 6 percent of Alcoa's mining and refining assets; 100 percent of Reynolds's farming assets, and all the lands apart from those on which mining facilities are located; 51 percent of both Reynolds's and Kaiser's mining assets and 7 percent of Alcan's mining and refining operations.[70]

To manage its growing interest in the bauxite-alumina industry, the Jamaican government set up many new bureaucracies. The major agency, the Jamaican Bauxite Institute (JBI), was established in 1976 to monitor, research and advise the government in every area and phase of the industry.

In reaction to Jamaica's declining market share, the bauxite levy was lowered in 1979. The four essential principals of the new levy strucure were:

1. A gradual reduction in levy rate to minimize the impact on foreign exchange earnings in the early years.

2. The setting of absolute minimum quantities for each company to produce.

3. The provision of volume incentives for production over minimum quantities referred to above.

4. The provision for a review of the proposals on January 1, 1984, or when the price of aluminum reaches $.85/lb., whichever came first.[71]

The ushering-in of a new government was seen in 1980, the free-market-oriented Jamaican Labour Party (JLP) under the leadership of Edward Seaga. The JLP recognized the critical importance of the mining sector in its bitterly fought campaign and called for definitive steps to facilitate rapid expansion. JLP relations with the MNCs are markedly better than those of the socialist PNP.

As the Jamaican government now owns a large portion of the bauxite deposits, and with Jamaican reserves as they presently exist, Jamaica can support an output that doubles the tonnage currently produced. The new governmental policy addressed the increase in output of both bauxite and alumina, while contracts are being pursued for the government to supply alumina to Venezuela, Mexico and the Soviet Union. The U.S. stockpiling efforts have also resulted in an increased demand for Jamaican bauxite, indicating a temporary upswing in the demand for bauxite-alumina, although the long-run prospects are not favorable.[72]

Domestic Politics in Jamaica

After concentrating on the bauxite industry and its impact on the Jamaican economy, we must now trace the changes in the composition of the Jamaican GNP by various sectors over time, in order to ascertain the nature of structural changes in bauxite output, to see how Jamaica under various governments has been part of this process. Outside of the mining sector, the sector that has undergone the most change as a result of bauxite production is agriculture. In the period from 1950–80 the agricultural sector declined from 31.5 percent to a little over 10 percent of the total national product.[73] The agricultural sector became only one-third as important to the GNP by 1980 as it had previously been in 1950. This trend continued throughout the early 1980s, and today agriculture accounts for only 8 percent of the Jamaican GNP.

In the early- to mid-nineteenth century, Jamaican lowlands were occupied by large sugar and cattle estates. After emancipation, many of the freed slaves left these large estates and established small subsistence holdings in the surrounding hills. Two types of landholdings, large estates and peasant holdings, still exist. With bauxite companies owning large parcels of land and small family dwellings subdivided each generation, however, the distinction between large and small landholdings has grown. In 1970 45 percent of the land was held in 300 properties of at least 500 acres, while 15 percent of the farms were under 5 acres; an area generally viewed as too small to support a family.[74] In a period of less than 20 years the bauxite companies were able to buy up large portions of the best agricultural land for afforda- ble sums.

At one time during the early nineteenth century, Jamaica was the world's largest producer of sugar, yet there was a rapid decline in the output of sugar during the middle of that century. Because estates failed to improve cultivation and processing standards, combined with the emancipation of slaves, Jamaica found itself nearly out of the sugar business altogether.

During the mid-twentieth century, a slow comeback in this industry was evident, with a record output of 515,000 tons of sugar produced in 1965.[75] The industry remains very unstable, however, because of the dependence on weather conditions and difficulty of obtaining adequate field labor (some of whom have gone on to high-paying jobs in the mining industry). Until 1974 almost 50 percent of the total output of sugar was grown on the large plantations. After 1974, under the Manley government, many large estates transferred ownership of the land to local farmers and worker cooperatives as part of the longstanding political patronage system.

During the late 1970s and early 1980s Jamaica's agricultural production appeared to be in deplorable condition. Of the major products, only citrus and cocoa products showed even the slightest increase.[76] In 1980 sugar cane and banana crops de- clined by 8 percent and 52 percent respectively.[77] Bauxite had taken up the slack, but it has been plagued by cyclical move- ments in demand.

Factors leading to the failure in agricultural production have persisted for several years. These include the lack of planting material, limited amounts of imported inputs due to a shortage in foreign exchange, inclement weather, and vandalism. During 1979–80 natural disasters and plant disease again played havoc with the agricultural industry and took a considerable toll. For example, the entire agricultural sector was affected by Hurricane Allan in 1980, whose economic losses were established at $514 million.[78] Bauxite production could not offset losses of this magnitude.

Aside from the purchase of land by the MNC aluminum interests, internal migration within Jamaica due to the vast disparity in living standards between the urban and agricultural-rural areas was undoubtedly a factor in explaining the striking decline in the number of agricultural workers and the farm population as a whole. During 1943–80 the population of the Kingston metropolitan area grew by 85 percent while that of the whole island grew only 30.1 percent.[79] Dreams of job opportunities in the city attracted people from the countryside, especially from the smaller farms where incomes tended to be lowest. The combination of displacement due to bauxite mining and increased urbanization has affected Jamaican politics and social conditions considerably.

Tourism, another major industry within Jamaica, has also acted as a catalyst, drawing many rural Jamaicans into urban areas. With the large influx of foreign capital it draws into the country, tourism provides a great boost to the Jamaican economy. Estimates of tourist expenditure were J$77.9 million in 1970, an increase of over J$70 million from 1950.[80] By 1980 tourism accounted for less income, due to the PNP nationalization of hotels and the bad image Jamaica had gained in the world press.

The level of expenditure in the tourist industry places tourism with bauxite (the illegal marijuana trade may be as large as both combined) as the leading export industries in Jamaica. But as in the bauxite-alumina industry, there exists a considerable amount of cost within the tourist industry. In order for hotels to be competitive and cater to the North American or European visitor, many goods had to be imported. For example, approximately 70 percent of the food used by hotels is imported.[81] Advertising campaigns, either "A beach and a country" or "Come back to the way things used to be," accounted for large expenditures, most of which went to U.S. ad agencies.

In many ways tourism helped cement the dual nature of the Jamaican economy. The demonstrable effect of earning in the modern industrial sector raises the wage expectations of the average laborer. Many people now prefer to remain idle rather than be employed in lower-paying jobs, such as in agriculture. The disparity between agricultural laborers and bauxite workers is more than 200 percent but the bauxite industry does not employ many persons nationwide.

Agriculture has been displaced as Jamaica's leading export, and other modern products and services have increased in importance to the Jamaican economy, bauxite arguably first among all others. Whereas the agricultural sector is labor-intensive, drawing on the talents and size of the Jamaican population, bauxite mining and tourism evolved as much more capital-intensive industries with a high level of imported products needed to support each industry. Bauxite and tourism are viewed as the economic salvation of Jamaica by whatever government finds itself in power, even if their strategies for development radically differ.

LESSONS FROM THE JAMAICAN RAW MATERIALS CASE

Ever since Hobson, economic theorists have been interested in the specialization of countries in the export of raw materials. Lenin thought that the acquisition of raw materials was one of the principal manifestations of "monopoly capitalism." Marxists, including PNP officials in Jamaica, have seen the specialization of the developing countries in the supply of raw materials as part of their inherently "unequal position" in the system of exchange. That the developing countries are victims of the rich nations has been widely assumed, as has the assertion that specialization in supply of raw materials has an adverse effect on the economics of the developing countries. But both assumptions are unsupportable by fact.[82]

Marxists have developed the theory of the "gatekeeper effect," which claims that developed countries keep the underdeveloped countries in their position as suppliers of raw materials by dominating the LDCs' access to the outside world, controlling access to technology, capital, and resources necessary for industrialization. This supposedly prevents LDCs from becoming self-sufficient or able to export processed goods, thereby perpetuating the existing relationship. There is, however, also the possibility that managerial incompetence or political corruption in the developing countries' governments or private sectors could lead to the perpetuation of this specialization in the exporting of raw materials, or the adverse economic consequences these countries face.

There are several processes which underlie the assumed negative effect of specialization in the export of raw materials on economic development including:

1. The historical pattern dating back to the sixteenth century. The world division of labor, which was started with slavery, is still seen as a cause of contemporary world inequality.

2. International demand for raw materials is viewed as basically inelastic. Therefore, improvements in productivity of raw material exporters which result in increased supply confront a nearly fixed demand and lower unit prices.

3. Raw materials price fluctuation makes it difficult for government planners or entrepreneurs to make rational economic plans. This situation is often aggravated by the fact that the external trade flows of underdeveloped countries is a larger portion of their GNP than it is for developed countries. (In investigating the link between economic growth and raw-material specialization from the perspective of price instability, however, significant relationships between export price instability and economic growth rates are nonexistent.)

4. Production financed by foreign interests whereby the export of raw materials results in net outflows of cash.

5. Specialization in raw materials trade allocates national resources in a way that is less than optimal from a growth standpoint. Specifically, it is alleged that this specialization hinders investment in social and economic sectors that are likely to have multiplier effects on the developing country's economy.

This collection of five Marxist arguments, which form the basis of the "gatekeeper theory," assert that specialization in raw materials trade adversely affects overall economic well-being. These arguments are, however, supported by very little real empirical evidence of a general or specific variety. The case of Jamaican bauxite itself can be used to disprove parts of the theory.

There is no reason to ignore the consequences and influence of internal processes on the development of underdeveloped countries, including Jamaica. Domestic considerations are not exclusively consequences of the country's position in the wider world-system. The conditions under which terms of trade can be influenced and modified by actions of the exporting LDCs also need to be explored. The elites that influence the economies within the underdeveloped world do so by managing internal factors. These factors are also important in the development of national, especially Third World, economies. The transformation of wealth accruing from exports into industrial development is influenced by national information capacity, which is largely independent of the degree of processing of a country's exports. Whether a country specializes in raw material exports like bauxite or processed exports is not necessarily the only important factor in its economic development.

What is undebatable is U.S. interest in both Jamaica and the Caribbean region as a whole, not only because of its raw materials. The U.S. national interest is threatened not only by supply disruptions of an important mineral—bauxite—but by the influence and potential threat of less than friendly regimes in the area whose boundaries form the third border of the United States and whose sealanes are of vital importance to U.S. economic and military security.

Under the socialist PNP regime in Jamaica, moves were afoot that not only enabled the Jamaican government to have an enlarged voice in the bauxite industry but also increased relations with Cuba, the area's Soviet proxy. With the election of the JLP in 1980, and the bauxite stockpiling efforts of the U.S. government soon thereafter, it appeared that the U.S. had strengthened its role not only in the production process of a vital and strategic mineral but had also, possibly more notably, cemented its position vis-a-vis the free enterprise Seaga government, in what now appears to be a capitalistic developing country.

The U.S. Department of State in February 1982 gave further evidence of U.S. involvement in Jamaica. Feeling the rising threat of communism in the Caribbean Basin, the United States addressed the need to check the communist drive for power, as "the future could well bring more Cubas: totalitarian regimes so linked to the Soviet Union that they become factors in the military balance, and so incompetent economically that their citizens only hope becomes that of one day migrating to the United States."[83]

By looking at the bauxite-alumina industry in Jamaica, we can see the mutual interests of the MNCs, developing countries, and the U.S.-Jamaican involvement in the industry cannot be undone, and certainly represents more than a symbol of token national participation, reflecting an increasingly active role in bauxite production. However, the United States, because of its proven economic and national security interests in Jamaica, and particularly in her strategically important bauxite reserves, should not take lightly potential supply disruptions at the source, total nationalization of the industry, or flirtation with communist nations and economic systems. These pose definite direct and indirect risks to the United States itself.

VULNERABILITY AND SECURITY OF SUPPLY

Several factors influence the supply and consumption of raw materials (as was noted in our Jamaican case study) including: existing deposits, availability of capital and technology, sufficient energy supplies, transportation infrastructure, industrial and military demand, and export potential. But the overriding factor is political power—which controls exploratory rights, labor costs and availability, environmental restitution, capital investment, energy supply, rights of way, taxation, import and export duties, foreign trade organizations, the use of the military and development.

Bohdan O. Szuprowicz in *How to Avoid Strategic National Shortages* lists twenty danger points to consider for any given mineral:

1. Single supply source.
2. Lack of domestic reserve.
3. Lack of substitute materials.
4. Immediate world reserves.
5. High import dependence.
6. Supplies by allocation.
7. Price controls.
8. Energy requirements.

9. Irregular and infrequent supplies.

10. Import/export controls.

11. Environmental restrictions on use.

12. Health and safety impacts on production.

13. Very high military usage.

14. Declining use of material.

15. Technological development threat.

16. Low volume of total sales.

17. Low level of production.

18. Poor usage visibility.

19. Low recycling potential.

20. High existing or potential taxation.[84]

Bauxite-aluminum is affected to some degree by numbers 2, 5, 8, 10, 11, 12, 13, and 20 on the above list. Using Keohane and Nye's definition, the U.S. economy is sensitive (that is, vulnerable) to the exent it is open to costly effects imposed from outside before policies can be introduced to change the situation.[85] The extent to which bauxite-aluminum falls into this sensitive category depends on how affected the particular danger points are in any given instance.

There exists most definitely a close integration of military and economic spheres in any definition of U.S. national security. The chairman of the U.S. Joint Chiefs of Staff has been quoted as describing "our current military commitment to forty-one foreign countries as entirely consistent with our dependence on free-flowing international trade, and the forward development of our military forces continues to support these important economic interests."[86]

A secure access to needed supplies such as bauxite is an overriding concern of private capital, military, and political sectors in the United States. A 20 percent aluminum shortage would reduce the U.S. GNP by approximately 3 percent. Because aluminum ranked 28th in military share of U.S. national consumption of natural resources and major end-users, or 5.8 percent of the total, we are presented with an item of some strategic significance.[87] In fact, it can be argued that "Aluminum has become the most important single bulk material of modern warfare. . . . No war can be carried to a successful conclusion today without using and destroying vast quantities of aluminum. . . . We must plan the aluminum capacity available to the whole free world of nations strictly in terms of this awful prospect."[88]

Since the United States, Canada, Japan, and Western European countries are the major producers and consumers of aluminum outside of the centrally planned economies, the heavy dependence of these nations for bauxite and aluminum imports cannot be taken lightly.

If we were to estimate accurately the probability of disruption in bauxite supplies we would need to assess deliberate actions on the part of foreign governments or the IBA, civil disorders in producing states, military conflict in areas surrounding or including producing states, possible demand surges, and natural disasters. Other real threats include the demands of the New International Economic Order (NIEO),[89] international commodity agreements, terrorism, sabotage, transportation and shipping disruptions, labor costs, strikes, boycotts, new legislation, and especially taxation.

Clearly, the economic problems arising from bauxite-aluminum interdependence are security problems because vital U.S. interests and values are constantly threatened by adverse foreign actions or events. These circumstances place three major demands on government, according to Klaus Knorr: (1) demands for direct public action to reduce or eliminate adverse foreign economic imports; (2) demands for a redistribution of the perceived burden of adjusting to foreign events, or for toleration of direct redistributive action; and (3) demands for a redistribution of the perceived burden of national measures designed to cope with adverse foreign imports.[90] Whether the United States has the political will to bear the costs or seek relief through various actions, thereby managing or mitigating the effects of potential disturbances, remains to be seen.

Precise vulnerability is always difficult to gauge. We lack sufficient and exact information about which minerals and commodities will be most necessary and what disruptions in one mineral would imply across the sectors of the U.S. economy. The implications for national vulnerability stemming from a potential bauxite-aluminum crisis are many, and overall vulnerability must aggregate these implications. According to a study by Resources For the Future (RFF), the principal threat, of the many potential threats, to U.S. and NATO supplies of bauxite is "the possibility that production in the Caribbean will be disrupted by internal strife or military conflict with neighboring states."[91]

Another factor to consider in estimating strife in the acutely endangered Caribbean Basin, or elsewhere, is Soviet activity.

SOVIET BEHAVIOR

Production of aluminum in the Sino-Soviet bloc has experienced an annual growth of nearly 19 percent. The Soviet Union cannot satisfy its present needs, and, therefore, plans extensive expansion. Deficiencies in bauxite ore will be satisfied by imports from Greece, Guinea, and Ghana, as well as from nonbauxite ores such as nepheline, alumite, and sillimanite.[92] Comecon has repeatedly advocated long-range agreements with Third World countries, including bauxite producers. The Soviet Union itself has established mining and processing plants supplying large quantities of minerals for development assistance. "Soviet promoters have offered technical assistance in the fora of geological surveys and have already engaged in a mineral reserves studies for many countries and actually explored in 15 of them. . . . New sources are of primary interest to Soviet planners."[93]

The worst-case scenario of a "resource war" in strategic minerals is by now well known. That the United States and its allies are headed to a likely collision with the Soviet Union over access to certain minerals, which would tighten world supplies, drive prices up, and mean spot shortages, has been documented. Daniel I. Fine, of M.I.T., among others, foresees a struggle with the Soviets over critical materials for which the West relies heavily on imports. He believes, "It is more like the beginning of a historic shift. The mineral resource balance of the USSR is following oil with a new era of less–than–self sufficiency."[94]

The Soviets seem to be acting simultaneously to gain military footholds in places where they would be able to cut off or disturb Western access to minerals, including bauxite, while they move into Third World mining, negotiating either on their own, or through the Eastern Bloc Council of Mutual Economic Assistance (CMEA). According to *Fortune*, "More than 27 technical and economic-assistance agreements with third world countries that produce strategic minerals or have deposits" have been signed.[95] Recently, the U.S. Department of State also investigated reports that French and West German companies negotiated a major contract with the Soviet Union in apparent violation of allied sanctions imposed after the invasion of Afghanistan. The project was a $1 billion aluminum smelter in Siberia. Originally Alcoa, a U.S. firm, was also to be involved but it withdrew after President Carter announced a ban on strategic exports.[96]

Soviet policy in the area of international trade poses a direct and real threat to U.S. bauxite-alumina supplies. As a world trade power the Soviet Union increasingly has the ability to worsen the U.S. and NATO materials position. The more obviously threatening Soviet behavior, however, is its direct and indirect action and influence in the Caribbean Basin, and in other vital sealanes where bauxite-alumina is shipped.

A UNIDO paper documents the rapid growth in shipments of bauxite and alumina, up more than 80 percent since 1966.[97] The importance of Australia and the security of the Pacific Basin in this regard is not to be ignored. A NATO–like military alliance is one prominent solution to provide the United States and NATO with more secure sources of strategic materials and shipping routes in the Pacific region. This "trioceanic concept" has definite validity given increased Marxist control and influence in Central America and the Caribbean, where major bauxite producers are located. It is not likely that the Soviet Union, or its proxy-states, would directly disrupt our supply routes over bauxite but annoying threats to the Panama Canal and north-south shipping lanes, strategic to the entire Western world, nonetheless persist. Recall that both Grenada and Jamaica under Manley made overtures to Comecon to become associate members. As one noted analyst summarized the point,

The political fragmentation, economic uncertainty, rising expectations and influence of Cuba combine to make the Caribbean a volatile region with trends towards more leftist and pro-communist regimes. The major and stated interest of the Soviet Union in Latin America is Cuba, and its existence as a communist military and political power on the doorsteps of the U.S. remains.[98]

Actual Soviet military presence may be limited in the region but the Soviets were able to establish a military presence in Cuba after 1961 and today they enjoy modern docking facilities, air bases, submarine facilities, satellite stations, and sophisticated intelligence operations for monitoring the U.S. Soviet strength has definitely increased in the Caribbean Basin and poses a real and potential threat.

Indeed, of the nine major sealanes:

1. Across the Mediterranean;
2. Via the Indian Ocean and Eastern Atlantic;
3. The Eastern Atlantic;
4. Across the Indian Ocean onward via the Eastern Atlantic;
5. Eastward across the Atlantic to Western Europe;
6. Across the Asian waters east of Malacca;
7. Eastward across the Indian Ocean and through the Malacca Straits;
8. From the Eastern Atlantic onward across the the Indian Ocean;
9. Westward across the Pacific;[99]

many are important for the transportation of bauxite-alumina or aluminum. Of these routes, 4, 5, and 9 are most vital relative to supply, commodity importance, and percentage of total supply transported by sea to importing countries, in the United States or Western Europe.

If historical records provide any guidance, there is something to be learned from the fact that before World War II U.S. ships carrying bauxite ore moved freely to North American ports but after December 7, 1941 German U-boats destroyed 25 percent of the fleet carrying the raw material for war planes and other U.S. defense items.[100]

SECTOR BY SECTOR ANALYSIS

Whether the United States is vulnerable to the Soviet Union, the IBA, Jamaica, or to another particular bauxite producer state, or to all simultaneously, what are the possible results of a bauxite disruption of some longevity? How vulnerable are various U.S. industries? Which industries would be most impacted?

Present end uses of aluminum by percent are: building 24.9 percent, transportation 25.3 percent, electric 12.1 percent, consumer durables 9.6 percent, containers 8.7 percent, equipment 8 percent, and other uses 11.4 percent. The building sector comprises end uses including: windows, doors, screens, wires, cables, siding, roofing, and duct work. Transportation includes cars, commercial vehicles, aircraft missiles, rail and marine. Consumer durables include appliances, utensils, furniture, refrigeration, and air conditioning. Electrical includes transmission and wires. Containers include foil, sheet, and cans. Future demand is proven in areas such as the auto industry, packaging electrical industry, and pipe.[101]

In another study of the aluminum industry, military-related end use of aluminum was estimated as 29.8 percent of total use, and chemicals and photography was also listed as a prominent end user at 5.9 percent.[102]

Alcoa, the largest company in the aluminum industry, lists its principal classes of products as: chemical products, primary aluminum products, flat rolled products, extruded, rolled and drawn products, other products; and its finished products as: packaging and containing, transportation, electrical, building and construction, and other products.

The major markets, sector-by-sector, for aluminum end-use products are then

Aircraft—wing skins and external fuel tanks.

Automobiles and trucks—bumpers, manifold heads, body sheet panels, intake manifolds, steering gear housing, wheels, alternator housings, differential housings, air conditioners and radiators. Trucks use aluminum in cabs, fuel tanks, chassis supports, floors, and wheels.

Chemicals—electrical insulators, space vehicle shields and nosecones, china, paper, aluminum fluoride, alum, sodium aluminate, titanium dioxide, and fire retardant in plastics, rubber, fiberboard, and cellulose insulation.

Consumer durables—tubing, refrigerators, freezers, air conditioners, and kitchen utensils.

Stadium and other seating—seats, railing, and pedestrian bridges.

Housing—siding, doors, windows, conservation improvements.

Railroads—unit trains, dining cars.

Distributors—sheet, plate, extrusions, wire, rods and bars for mill products.

Farming—roofing, silos, siding.

Powder and paste—biodegradable detergent, explosives, pigment for paints and coating.

Beverage—beer, wine, soft drink and distilled liquors use a variety of container and packaging requiring aluminum.

Tobacco and confectionery—foil.

Pharmaceutical—packaging.

Solar—hot water systems.

Food service—over 400 items.

Photography—film.

General purpose packaging—both food and nonfood products.

Food and Household—containers, foil, and laminated cartons.

Consumer—foil, bags, freezer paper, and containers.

Electrical—radiant cure insulation lines, wire, conductors and cables.[103]

This sector-by-sector analysis of aluminum industry end uses allows us to see the widespread effect to the U.S. economy in the unlikely event of a sustained bauxite-alumina cutoff or embargo. The entire spectrum of U.S. industry would in time be affected and sizable dislocation, plant closings and unemployment would ensue.

Of particular interest is the effect of such a cutoff on defense-related industry itself. The concept of a defense-industry vulnerability index has been developed and applied to the aircraft industry. Although aluminum was more secure than cobalt, it was found to be more vulnerable than titanium.

Realization of the foreign sources for most strategic minerals important to U.S. military power has by now been finally documented. As Allegheny International's Vice President E.E. Andrews relates, "The national security and the economic survival of the United States depend upon the nation's capability to secure an uninterrupted flow of critical minerals from politically unstable third world nations."[104] In fact, 41 percent of the weight of the B–1 bomber is aluminum alloy and F–15 fighters have Pratt and Whitney F–100 power plants, which require 7,020 lbs. of aluminum along with other strategic metals to construct.[105] Szuprowicz lists major military uses of critical materials and finds aluminum essential for aircraft, cartridge casings, missiles, and satellites. The U.S. Army War College also notes aluminum as a prominent metal in its Vulnerability Index. About 4 percent of total aluminum consumption goes to production of exclusively military goods. These account for 84 percent of all the aluminum that U.S. firms consumed in producing defense goods. This increasing use of aluminum focuses on its mobility, lightness in air transport, toughness in armor plating and substitution for steel in airframes and missiles.

In the event of a severe and protracted disruption of bauxite and aluminum, key U.S. industries could fail, and defense industries in particular would be harshly affected. The total aluminum-related industry presently accounts for $213,981 million in the U.S. economy, or 8.1 percent of the GNP, employing 6,944,800 persons or 7.6 percent of the entire U.S. workforce.

REMEDIES

The magnitude of the effect to the U.S. economy of a bauxite-alumina cutoff depends on many things, but could be short-circuited to a degree by active substitution, use of stockpiles, conservation, and intensified recycling of scrap. It is difficult to conceive a truly comprehensive national materials policy, but each group of materials, including metals, require legislation so as to overcome instability and vulnerability of supply. The guidelines of the U.S. Trade Act of 1974, which concerns export controls and access to supplies, as well as retaliatory measures in the form of trade concessions, should be expanded to include presidential power to cut off assistance, suspend credits, and even control U.S. investments. Mutually acceptable terms with primary bauxite suppliers—in the Caribbean and elsewhere—is mandatory. The foreign policy of the United States in particular its attention to social, racial, national, and developmental problems in areas of bauxite production, can help to alleviate potential interruptions. Fostering free-market economies that are dominated by the private sector is one way to forestall many of these political problems. However, the United States should not necessarily ignore or assist developing countries as the shift of smelting and refining capacity out of the country continues unabated. This downstreaming has deleterious ramifications for U.S. supply in the event of political instability or cartelization in the future.

Other primary remedies are material substitution and stockpiling. Each deserves our immediate attention. The United States may not be exactly what the chairman of United Technologies Corporation called "a have-not nation when it comes to critical materials," but we presently find ourselves in a dangerous situation, should a combination of events have an impact on either exporting countries or vital access routes. In fact, the United States is in a better situation than the rest of NATO as "most of our allies, including Britain and Japan, have virtually no government stockpiles at all."[106] This lack of preparedness on the part of our allies warrants neither our support nor emulation.

Substitution of other types of bauxite with different sources is a possible short-term solution to an unexpected cutoff. Even though "better grades of bauxite occur chiefly in tropical areas as a result of the weathering of volcanic rock, aluminum is present in clays elsewhere, and some of these can be substituted for bauxite in the production of aluminum, although at substantially higher cost, should the need arise."[107] Perhaps the United States should diversify its supply even further to include the introduction of these lower-grade bauxites which could act as a safety valve in the case of catastrophe. Certain U.S. aluminum companies have also claimed that exploitation of nonbauxite U.S. resources could be made profitable. Such experimentation should be supported. National Southwire is testing a pilot plant for production of alumina from alunite; Anaconda is interested in clays, especially Georgia kaolin; Alcoa is investigating anorthosite and coal-tailings as sources; while Pechiney is building a commercial-scale plant using a shale-based process to produce aluminum.[108]

Conservation has been studied by the Office of Technology Assessment, and numerous technical options can be outlined. Of particular interest are major redistribution, metal substitution, use of nonmetallic coating, product remanufacturing, re-cycling, product reuse, use of stocks, reduction of dissipative uses, reduction of milling losses, different forms of construction, allocations, reduction of postconsumer waste, export control, elimination of unnecessary metal in products and increase of product life.

Recycling or increased secondary-supply recovery, while only a small contributor to a shortfall, must also be enhanced. Scrap represents short-run net additions to the total supply, even though it accounts for only 3.5 percent of aluminum consumption.[109] Actually, 70 percent of the metals mined each year are lost, and less than 0.001 percent remains after ten cycle uses. Recycling extends the life of aluminum by less than ten years. However, more effective recycling measures could add more time. If consumption were reduced by only 0.5 percent per year, the life of the aluminum resource base, given the present recycling base, would be extended by over 100 years.[110]

While attending to our primary military needs as end-use aluminum consumers, the United States needs to better coordinate its public policies toward the national goal. Besides reducing U.S. dependency on foreign bauxite and alumina producers, tax policies should be considered that encourage substitution, conservation and recycling, and private stockpiles. Research and development should be funded in these areas and in seabed mining. The United States should also plan for a better national use of public lands, and most important, secure and manage our national strategic stockpile.

Satellite monitoring of shipping routes should continue, with the protection of vital lanes the most crucial task. The implications for national security of access and shipping of bauxite, and other raw materials and goods, falls on the U.S. Navy, and its force must be sufficient to deter potential threats, protect allies and trade partners, and deny control of critical passages to enemies or potentially threatening nations.

Overall, national security demands both efficiency of the private market in anticipating market changes, and a major role for the federal government as specified by the U.S. Strategic Stockpile Act, and the Strategic and Critical Materials Stockpiling Act of 1979.

Presently, the U.S. Strategic Stockpile consists of 62 mineral groups (and individual minerals), metals, and industrial materials. According to law the stockpile must be capable of supporting U.S. defense requirements: during a major war; for a three-year period; and assuming large-scale industrialization. It must also provide for a broad range of civilian economic needs. Decisions concerning the quantity and type of materials to be held in the National Defense Stockpile are the responsibility of FEMA. This agency has been criticized for poor planning and inefficiency, both of which must be overcome.

Until November 24, 1981, government stocks remained at 9,001,000 metric tons of Jamaican-type bauxite ore, 5,385,000 tons of Surinam-type ore, and 177,401 tons of calcined refractory-grade bauxite. The Federal stockpiles held no alumina, except as aluminum oxide abrasive grain and fused crude.[111] On November 24, 1981, President Reagan announced the purchase of 1.6 million tons of Jamaican bauxite for stocks. Reagan's statement intimated that the U.S. stockpile was "12 million tons short of the ore, which is critical to industries that are essential to support a mobilization effort."[112]

The efficacy of the present stockpile in the aluminum group depends in a crisis situation on the duration of supply disruption and the timing of substitution, conservation and recycling measures. However, a one-year embargo would reduce aluminum consumption by 45 percent. With stocks sufficient to the one-year consumption rate, a two-year embargo would not necessarily reduce consumption markedly. A larger stockpile is, however, a substantial deterrent against losses. Because short-run escalation of prices and potential embargoes are so uncertain and unannounced, policymakers should consider increasing the U.S. stockpile in bauxite and alumina as a defense against even the worst cases and all possible contingencies.

National security claims adhere when basic societal values and goods are perceived to be threatened by adverse foreign economic or military actions or events. In the interdependent global market of bauxite-alumina, potential threats exist and can be expected to intensify, given the level of interpenetration and mutual sensitivity among the national economies involved. These threats can, however, be managed and controlled, given proper attention and policies.

NOTES

1. Alfred Cowles, *The Story of Aluminum* (Chicago: Henry Regnery Co., 1958), p. 3.

2. For a geographical overview, see Albert S. Carlson, *Economic Geography of Industrial Materials* (New York: Reinholt Publishing Corp., 1956).

3. Ida Valeton, *Bauxite* (Amsterdam: Elsevier Publishing Co., 1972), p. 11.

4. F. E. Hamilton, "Aluminum Is Power," *Geographical Maqazine*, 21 (June 1979), pp. 593–600.

5. For historical background see Percy W. Bidwell, *Raw Materials: A Study of American Policy* (New York: Harper and Row, 1958).

6. Isaiah A. Litvak and Christopher J. Maule, "The International Bauxite Agreement: A Commodity Cartel in Action," *International Affairs*, 56 (Spring 1980), p. 296.

7. "Bauxite and Alumina," *U.S. Bureau of Mines Minerals Yearbook*, 1981, p. 4.

8. Douglas Woods and James C. Burrows, *The World Aluminum-Bauxite Market* (New York: Praeger Publishers, 1980), p. 46.

9. "Aluminum," *U. S. Bureau of Mines Bulletin 1980*, p. 671.

10. Ibid.

11. See *The Economist*, April 7, 1979, p. 79.

12. *Business Week*, October 19, 1981, p. 97.

13. S.R. Spector, "Short-Medium-and-Long Range Trends in Aluminum Supply and Demand," *UNIDO* Paper, May 1978, p. 19. See also James Zambo, "Bauxite and Alumina Production," *UNIDO* Paper, May 1978, which discusses and assesses technologies for making alumina.

14. See *Problems and Prospects of the Primary Aluminum Industry*, OECD (Paris), 1973.

15. *Business Week*, February 26, 1979, p. 109. See also *Business Week*, September 25, 1978, p. 116.

16. See *Industrial Adaptation in the Primary Aluminum Industry*, OECD (Paris), 1976.

17. James H. Cobbe, *Governments and Mining Companies in Developing Countries* (Boulder, CO: Westview Press, 1979), p. 27.

18. *Multinational Business*, no. 1 (1979), p. 35.

19. Ibid., p. 36.

20. Wilfred Malenbaum, *World Demand for Raw Materials in 1985–2000* (New York: McGraw-Hill for Mining Information Services, 1980).

21. See Ferdinand E. Banks, *Bauxite and Aluminum: An Introduction to*

the Economics of Nonfuel Minerals (Toronto: Lexington Books, 1979). This comprehensive work inspects all the economic aspects of the aluminum group including profit, exploration, processing, and trade. Graphs on bauxite capacity are illuminating.

22. *Mineral Development in the Eighties: Prospects and Problems*, A report of the British-North American Committee (New York, 1976), p. 3.

23. Ibid., p. 17.

24. See "The Economic Effects of Pollution Controls on the Non-Ferrous Metals Industry," prepared for the Council on Environ-Quality by Charles River Associates, 1974.

25. *International Minerals Cartels and Embargoes: Policy Implications for the U.S.*, prepared by Charles River Associates (New York: Praeger Publishers, 1980), p. 44.

26. Ibid., p. 48.

27. Ibid., pp. 110–11.

28. Woods and Burrows, p. 175.

29. Hu Gentles, "Bauxite Alumina Perspectives," *The Gleaner*, November 21, 1980, p. 36.

30. The White House, Office of the Press Secretary, Statement of the President, November 24, 1981.

31. *Jamaica Bauxite Annual Report*, "Jamaica and the World Aluminum Industry in 1979," 1979.

Some factors affecting performance of industry outside of Jamaica include:

1. Occurence of long-term U.S. recession.

2. Performance of other major market areas.

3. Effectiveness of price controls in the U.S. and the extent of metal exportation.

4. Outcome of wage negotiations in U.S. aluminum industry.

5. Extent of aluminum stock rebuilding.

6. Power availability in the U.S. Pacific Northwest.

32. *Encyclopedia Americans*, "Bauxite," 1981.

33. "Jamaican" Fact Sheet 81, p. 7.

34. Gentles, p. 36.

35. John MacPherson, *Caribbean Lands* (Longman Caribbean Ltd. Essex, 1981), p. 45.

36. Ibid.

37. Carlton E. Davis, "Jamaica in the World Aluminum Industry II," *The JBI Journal* (July 1981), p. 101.

38. Ibid.

39. Ibid., p. 114. See also *Economic and Social Survey of Jamaica*, "Mineral Industry," 1980.

40. Gentles, p. 36.

41. "Aluminum by Alcoa," p. 14.

42. "Reynolds Metals—Annual Report 1980," p. 19.

43. Ibid.

44. Ibid., p. 19.

45. I.A. Litvak and C.J. Maule, "Transnational Corporations in the Bauxite-Aluminum Industry: With Special Reference to the Carribean," ECLA/CTC Joint Unit Paper (July 1977), p. 1.

46. "Jamalco," Jamaica Bauxite Mining Ltd./Alcoa Minerals of Jamaica, 1980.

47. Gentles, p. 36.

48. Michael Manley, *The Politics of Change* (Washington, D.C.: Howard University Press, 1975), p. 259.

49. "The Aluminum Industry in 1980," *The JBI Journal* (July 1981), p. 66.

50. Ibid.

51. Ibid.

52. Ibid., p. 66.

53. "Aluminum by Alcoa," Company Report, 1980.

54. Aluminum Company of America 1980 Annual Report.

55. Aluminum Industry in 1980," p. 63.

56. "Jamalco," Company Report, 1980.

57. "Aluminum Industry in 1980," p. 63.

58. Litvak and Maule, p. 63.

59. "Jamalcan," Fact Sheet, 1981.

60. "Aluminum Industry in 1980," p. 62.

61. Ibid.

62. Litvak and Maule, p. 99.

63. "Aluminum Industry in 1980," p. 64.

64. Reynolds Metals Annual Report 1980.

65. Litvak and Maule, p. 89.

66. Ibid., pp. 89–90.

67, Manley, p. 255. See "The Bauxite (Production Levy) Act," *The Jamaican Gazette*, vol. CII, no. 62, October 22, 1979.

68. Manley, ibid., p. 260.

69. Gentles, p. 36. Two articles that represent this sentiment are: Norman Girvan, "Why We Need to Nationalize Bauxite, and How" in Norman Girvan (ed.), *Readings in Political Economy of the Caribbean* (Kingston: New World Group, Ltd., 1977), pp. 217–40; and Carl Stone, "Bauxite and National Developments in Jamaica" in Aggrey Brown (ed.), *European Power and Change in Jamaica* (Kingston: Jamaica Publishing House, 1977), pp. 136–41.

70. "Mineral Industry," *Economic and Social Survey of Jamaica*, 1980, pp. 7.1–7.2.

71. "Jamaica and the World Aluminum Industry in 1971," p. 7.

72. Ibid., p. 8. In reply to this purchase, Mr. Seymour Mullings, leader of the appointed PNP on Business, said, "The country has been temporarily accommodated by a good god-father and three cheers for that, but I don't know if it is good for the country to rest its hope for survival on a good daddy." *Sunday Gleaner*, November 29, 1981.

73. Owen Jefferson, *The Post-War Economic Development of Jamaica* (Kingston, Jamaica: Institute of Social and Economic Research, 1972), p. 49.

74. MacPherson, p. 48.

75. Ibid., p. 48.

76 "Economic Activity 19890 in Caribbean Countries," *A United Nations Report*, p. 4.

77. Ibid.

78. Ibid.

79. Jefferson, p. 16.

80. Ibid., p. 177.

81. Ibid.

82. Jacques Delacroix, "Study of Raw Materials and Economic Growth: A Cross-National Study," *American Sociological Review* (October 1977), pp. 795–806.

83. "Democracy and Security in the Caribbean Basin," *Department of State News Release*, Policy No. 364, p. 5.

84. Bohdan 0. Szuprowicz, *How to Avoid Strategic Materials Shortages* (New York: John Wiley and Sons, 1981), p. 8.

85. As quoted in Helge Hveem, "Militarization of Nature: Conflict and Control Over Strategic Resources and Some Implications for Peace Policies," *Journal of Peace Research* (V, SVI, 1979), p. 7.

86. Ibid., p. 1.

87. Ibid., p. 23.

88. P. Anderson, *Aluminum for Defense and Prosperity* (Washington, D.C.: Public Affairs Institute, 1951), p. 4.

89. See Samuel K. Asante, "Restructuring Transnational Mineral Agreements," *American Journal of International Law* (July 1979), pp. 335–71.

90. Klaus Knorr and Frank N. Trager (eds.), *Economic Issues and National Security* (Lawrence, Kansas: University of Kansas Press), p. 7.

91. Woods and Burrows, p. 510.

92. "Aluminum in the Sino-Soviet Bloc," Central Intelligence Agency, January 1962.

93. Szuprowicz, p. 88.

94. As quoted in *Fortune*, July 28, 1980, p. 43.

95. Ibid., p. 44.

96. *New York Times*, August 16, 1981, p. 27.

97. John Brandon, Graham Hadin, and Peter Rowbotham, "Transport of Bauxite and Alumina: Volume, Costs, Technical Background, and Future Trends," *UNIDO* Paper, May, 1978. See also "Transnational Corporations in the Bauxite/Aluminum Industry," *U.N. Centre for Transnational Corporations*, pp. 11 and 16, for tables on world seaborne trade in bauxite and alumina.

98. Szuprowicz, p. 138. See also *Strategic Minerals: A Resource Crisis* (Washington, D.C.: CENS, 1981) which provides President Reagan's address, "Central America: Defending Our Vital Interests," April 27, 1982, U.S. Department of State, Current Policy 482, applies.

99. Yuan-li Wu, *Raw Material Supply in a Multipolar World* (New York: Crane Russak and Co., 1979).

100. James E. Sinclair and Robert Parker, *The Strategic Metals War* (New York: Arlington House, 1983), p. 94.

101. Sterling Brubaker, *Trends in the World Aluminum Industry* (Baltimore: Johns Hopkins Press, 1967), p. 30.

102. Ronald Graham, *The Aluminum Industry and the Third World: Multinational Corporations and Underdevelopment* (London: Zed Press, 1982), p. 49. See also S. Moment, "Long-Term Association of Developing Countries with Consumers of Bauxite, Alumina, and Aluminum," *UNIDO Paper*, May 1978; Mr. Racketzki and S. Zorm, *Financing Mining Projects in Developing Countries* (London: Mining Journal Books, 1979); and E. Balaza and I. Molnar, "Bauxite, Alumina, Aluminum: Main Factors for Decision-Making on Industrial Development," *UNIDO* Paper, May, 1978. This is a cogent study of factors on investment including: natural resources, conditions, technology, capital, markets, manpower, skill, government incentives, and regional cooperation.

103. Reynolds Metals Co., Background Data, 1981.

104. As quoted in *U.S. News and World Report*, February 8, 1982, p. 59.

105. Sinclair and Parker, p. 162. See also "Strategic Mineral Dependence: The Stockpile Dilemma," Georgetown University Center for Strategic and International Studies, 1979.

106. As quoted in *Fortune*, February 9, 1981, p. 68.

107. *Mineral Development in the Eighties: Prospects and Problems*, p. 3.

108. *International Minerals Cartels and Embargoes: Policy Implications for the U.S.*, p. 115.

109. *International Minerals Cartel and Embargoes: Policy Implications for the U.S.*, p. 126. 110. Hveem, p. 14.

110. Hveem, p. 14.

111. *U.S. Bureau of Mines Yearbook*, "Bauxite and Alumina," 1980, p. 5. See also Federal Emergency Management Agency, "Stockpile Report to the Congress," Washington, D.C., April-September 1980.

112. As quoted in the New York *Times*, November 25, 1981, p. 4.

II

Development Issues

8

The North-South Dialogue Reconsidered

THE PRESENT STATE OF AFFAIRS: A SLOW DEATH

From the 1964 United Nations Conference on Trade and Development (UNCTAD I), the first major North-South conference on development questions, economic negotiations in various UN forums have crystallized along geopolitical lines. It may have been inevitable that the developing countries would emerge in the 1960s as a group struggling to find their own identity in the process of decolonization. The real objective of the G–77, according to one of its founders, Julius Nyerere (as he phrased it when he spoke before the UN General Assembly in 1962), has always been "to complete the liberalization of the third world countries from external domination."

Since 1964, the Group of 77 (presently 128 members) has been the principal organ of the Third World for voicing its collective economic interests in the North-South dialogue. Most of these discussions have taken place within the United Nations system. The G–77 however has no permanent institutions or constitution. The informality of the Group has shown enough flexibility to absorb and accommodate the many diverging interests of its large membership.[1]

Until the early 1970s the G–77 tried to achieve its purposes by suggesting reforms of the international economic system that had evolved under the post-war Bretton Woods institutions. By the early 1970s LDC attitudes had changed. The decolonization process was complete; the cold war had subsided; international development efforts were viewed with disappointment; and grave doubts about prevailing development models were being voiced. Between 1970 and 1973 the Non-Aligned Movement (NAM) (at the level of heads of state) made development questions a priority issue.

The politicization of North-South issues commenced, most particularly in the May 1974 Declaration and Program of Action on the Establishment of a New International Economic Order (NIEO), and in the February 1979 Arusha Program for Collective Self Reliance and Framework for Negotiations. The NIEO was pushed in all UN agencies as an addition to the basic 1945 UN foundations—maintenance of international peace and global security. Third World development had emerged as an important challenge for the world community.

The NIEO-inspired resolutions that continue to surround all economic discussions in UN forums fall into five familiar categories:

1. Transfer of resources—proposals for increasing the flow of development assistance from developed to developing countries (to 0.7 percent of developed countries' GNP), with special aid for the least developed countries (LLDCs) and mitigation of debt burdens.

2. Science and technology—expanded assistance, technology transfer, increased research on LDC problems, cooperation on strengthening of infrastructure, policies to counter the brain drain, and various international codes.

3. Industrialization—redeployment of developed country industries to LDCs, and the encouragement of investment consistent with laws, regulations and needs of the developing countries (so-called TNC discussions).

4. Food and agriculture—trade policies to increase agricultural production and export earnings, increased food assistance and maintenance of food grain reserves.

5. International trade—significant changes to bring about price and income stability in a host of commodities as well as export promotion, including an integrated program of commodity agreements, the Common Fund, and greater Economic Cooperation between Developing Countries (ECDC).

Even into the mid–1980s the NIEO model has continued to underlie routine discussions between the developed and developing countries in such forums as UNCTAD, the United Nations Industrial Development Organization (UNIDO), the UN General Assembly (UNGA), the Economic and Social Committee of the UNGA (ECOSOC), other specialized UN agencies, and on occasion even in the International Monetary Fund (IMF) and World Bank (where the G–77 acts through the Group of 24).

Some have suggested that it may be time to reconsider, recast, or even end the North-South dialogue. Reconsideration would require focusing on what the South wants and what has led to its redundant and maximalist bargaining positions. The South has asserted without much moderation for over three decades

strong convictions that the present system is flawed by unequal exchanges, a monetary system with insufficient liquidity to meet the needs of the poor, and resource transfers that are altogether too limited;

determined calculations that a shift in power toward OPEC, G–77, the NAM and Southern regionalism would limit Northern power and dominance;

pleas for the necessity of structural change urging that the NIEO be adopted as a radical measure, with an element of "all or nothing" thinking; and

increasing frustration over the slow pace of change.

THE MOST PLAGUING PROBLEMS IN THE NORTH-SOUTH ARENA

Multilateral North-South negotiations, now three decades old, are at an all time low ebb. Some form of international economic negotiations on development and trade topics will likely continue into the 1990s, but the lessons learned so far suggest that a redirection is in the making, having implications for negotiating behavior, procedural guidelines, and conceivably even substantive development and trade issues. If North-South negotiations are not moved away from the present zero-sum game atmosphere evidenced in the never-ending NIEO-inspired proposals, some participants feel they could wither away.

There is no escaping the fact that the positions and expectations of the developed (North) and developing countries (South) have been fundamentally at odds. Negotiations have been full of exhortations and condemnations. Therefore any mutually beneficial future North-South negotiations would have to change the present environment. A more creative North-South dialogue conducted on a different footing and incorporating lessons from past negotiations could go some distance toward providing all parties with a greater possibility of acceptable outcomes. These lessons could lead the participants to a more cautious attitude about the prospects for instant success and could overcome a number of plaguing problems. Improvements could include:

an improved process—including better preparation and streamlining of meetings, seeking common definitions, and imposing greater structure;

a better information system—more statistical and technical data, an improved flow of information, and more informed, less biased studies;

the identification of real interests—formulae for agreements are necessary instead of confrontation; opportunities for trade-offs need to be found; deadlines need to be imposed; and

the breakdown of groups—the realities of international politics and economics cut across the established lines, so parties will have to begin to transcend the present divisions so as to form new alliances.

Even with these improvements critical changes would still need to occur in order to move North-South talks beyond their current stagnation. The most important and necessary changes revolve around questions of leadership, structure, and most certainly, the very group system that has come to define North-South negotiations.

Leadership

UNCTAD and many specialized UN agencies have had strong leaders in the past, often coming from the ranks of the radical G–77. This leadership cadre has led to biased secretariats, as well as personnel decisions that have allowed patronage and politicization. It is not surprising, therefore, that the question of new leadership has been raised since the end of Gamania Corea's term as secretary general of UNCTAD at the close of 1984.

The flood of paper issued by those UN secretariats dealing with economic questions is massive, uneven, technically deficient in quality, and grossly redundant. Management problems at UNCTAD and other UN agencies are widespread and have resulted, among other things, in excessive documentation, ideological reports, wasteful and duplicative programs, questionable financial management, and a poor flow of information.

Structure

The "dialogue process" as it has been called, has eroded to a shouting match, sometimes even a monologue. There is little else in many UN meetings on economic development besides the reading of speeches in condemnatory tones. The rancor and disorganization of UNCTAD Trade and Development Board meetings (TDBs), in the present format (twice yearly), and preparation for another general conference (UNCTAD VII in 1987) are evidence that present structures are not productive. The overlap of functions and redundancy of issues in various UN forums are further reasons why some suggest delimiting the North-South dialogue. Centralization of discussion within UNCTAD has been assumed by developing and developed countries, but this de facto situation is now being challenged, since UNCTAD does not have the expertise, or in a few cases the mandate, to deal with some of the issues it tries to handle.

The Group System

The G–77 is seen by its members as a kind of "trade union of the poor," a "unity of opposition" to the rich countries, and not necessarily a commitment to a single ideology. In their own words, the G–77 is based on a "shared historical experience, shared economic dependence, and a shared set of needs and aspirations" (Group of 77 Statement of Purpose, 1964).

Since the Ad Hoc Committee on Restructuring of the Economic and Social Sectors of the UN System (created by the UNGA in 1975), the G–77 has had twin goals: (1) to make the United

Nations responsive to the concerns of the majority, that is, developing countries; and (2) to increase the flow of resources generated by the UN system. The G–77 has sought to strengthen those agencies and institutions amenable to their interests. Therefore the UNGA was transformed into the main UN policymaking and negotiating forum. Three additional countries were added to the Advisory Committee on Administration and Budgetary Questions (ACABQ). UNCTAD was strengthened and new proposals for centering operational activities in the regional economic commissions were launched. A closer look at the present groups will provide us with a better assessment of why the North-South discussions have become so sterile and unproductive.

The Group of 77

The G–77 is not homogeneous or cohesive. Consensus in the group is increasingly difficult to maintain. Countries in the developing world vary culturally, ideologically, regionally, politically, and economically, and also by their level of development. Without permanent leadership, staff, headquarters, or a secretariat, responsibility for coordination of the G–77 has rotated annually. To date, Algeria, Argentina, Brazil, Cuba, Egypt, India, Indonesia, Jamaica, Mexico, Nigeria, Pakistan, the Philippines, Sri Lanka, Venezuela, and Yugoslavia have played prominent roles in the Group but have not dominated. Increasingly, the cleavages among the Latin American group (GRULA), those countries involved in the Lome Convention (countries in the African, Carribean, and Pacific region), the Newly Industrialized Countries (NICs), and the least developed countries (LLDCs primarily in Africa) have been accentuated. The success of OPEC has increased strains within the G–77, as has the formation of the Singapore group of more moderate LDCs. Indeed, some have even advocated that certain prosperous NICs be graduated from the G–77.[2]

The institutionalized group structure in UNCTAD decision-making has generally tended to blur national differences and exacerbate intergroup confrontation, especially between developed and developing nations. In this process some smaller developed countries (particularly Scandinavian ones) have tried without much success to play the role of mediators. Overall the group system has promoted inflexibility and increased the difficulty of compromise or meaningful, constructive dialogue. One Third World leader stated that the group system needs a thorough overhaul because of the antagonistic relationship it has engendered. In this individual's view,

Today, at meetings on any economic issue, it goes without saying that the developed and developing countries square off almost automatically, as if all their interests were diametrically opposed. What was initially true at UNCTAD has now spread throughout the UN system, with these inflexible groupings immobilizing the organization's entire economic negotiating machineries and rendering them virtually useless. (Attributed to an undisclosed ASEAN leader at the UNESCAP meetings, 1984)

This group structure has implications for intragroup decisionmaking as well. Within the G-77, for instance, a sort of democratization has resulted. In the interest of unity any small nation with a unique interest in any issue usually will be accommodated, especially by its regional group, provided it is vocal enough. When programs are brought to the group as a whole, compromises are rarely struck. Rather, policies are formulated on the basis of very general abstract principles, at the expense of substance. This lowest-common-denominator tactic has served to keep group solidarity intact, even while it is constantly being pulled apart by economic reality.

African influence within the G-77 is a particular problem because of the veto power the Africans have possessed as a result of sheer numbers. The Africans have generally been willing to make deals with Brazilian and Mexican efforts on international finance in return for support on African demands that flows of development aid on concessional terms be increased. Afro-Asian compromises, when they have been struck, have come in the areas of commodities and programs for the least developed countries.

Many African leaders provided some of the most inflammatory rhetoric in the North-South debate and have been in the forefront of those demanding a NIEO. This penchant for high-blown rhetoric has rarely translated into substance. African interest in Economic Cooperation among Developing Countries (ECDC) has been very forceful, given many African countries strongly held views on collective self-reliance. ECDC and TCDC (dealing with cooperation on technology issues) are now routinely part of UNCTAD and ECOSOC proceedings, largely on account of African insistence. Gamani Corea, former secretary general of UNCTAD, summed up the importance of ECDC when he said,

The concept of cooperation among developing countries is founded on two aspects. On the one hand it embodies the idea of mobilization of the capacity of the developing countries to act vis a vis their relationships with the rest of the world, to improve their part of collective bargaining; and secondly, it strengthens their ties with each other in the field of trade and other exchanges and does away with the predominantly bipolar relations between themselves and the metropolitan powers, which has been left to them as a legacy from the past.

Group B

Group B, the industrialized, developed countries of the so-called North (although the hemispheric reference is technically incorrect), is likewise a diverse collection of states with strong notions of sovereignty. Many of the Group B states appear to prefer the OECD and World Bank/IMF/GATT settings to those of the United Nations for the resolution of international economic problems. Recently, the World Bank Development Committee, for instance has been more fully used for many trade, development, and debt issues.

Most European and other Western countries have tried to accommodate Third World interests. There is, however, a movement on the part of many countries, due in part to the U.S. role and the experience at UNESCO, to be more realistic and pragmatic with regard to the overall North-South dialogue.

The *"Groupe de Reflexion,"* an informal working party in Group B, concerning the reform of UNCTAD, has been meeting in Geneva in recent years to suggest changes within that body.

Such topics as UNCTAD decisionmaking, organization of meetings, the group process, future work programs, negotiating techniques, and the role of the secretariat are presently under discussion. But changes that Group B wants may be hard to bring about because the G–77 members in UNCTAD generally (publicly at least) like UNCTAD the way it is—functioning as a de facto G–77 secretariat. Because of the stalemate evidenced by the entire North-South process, some LDCs privately recognize that the reform process now under way because of Group B pressure is long overdue and absolutely necessary.

Group D

The Group D bloc, the Soviet Union and East European countries (with the exception of Romania, which functions as part of the G–77) are increasingly irrelevant in North-South discussions. While the Soviets have tried to make political hay by joining the Third World in a critique of dependency and imperialism, they have on the whole been less than successful. The Soviets have failed to attract many LDCs to either a Soviet-style economic system or to an appreciation for the tenets of their ideology.

Increasingly, developing countries have become more cognizant of Group D stinginess on development assistance. For example, Western developed countries provided approximately 92 percent of the total contributions to UN development activities and programs; developing countries nearly 7 percent; and the Soviet Union and Eastern Europe, only 1 percent. On a per-capita basis, Western countries contributed roughly fifty times as much as Eastern ones ($1.49 versus $0.03). With this track record, documented by the UN itself, and a historical alibi that they are "not guilty" for the colonial experience, Group D collectively has come to play a minor part in the larger international economic discussion relating to Third World development.

RHETORIC VERSUS REALITY

Established 20 years ago to study the changing structure of trade in commodities, manufactured goods and services between the developing and industrialized nations, and providing advice on global questions related to finance, trade, development, and technology transfer, UNCTAD has not achieved prominence remotely comparable with the World Bank, the IMF, or GATT. Some think UNCTAD is ineffectual because it embodies the rhetoric, theories, and political influences that have dominated Third World thinking since the late 1960s. Politicizing economic questions from the outset, UNCTAD and other UN bodies have created a confrontational atmosphere with little chance for substantive discussions or pragmatic resolution of issues. Instead, the broken system of North-South mechanisms has become what one keen observer referred to as "at best, a cynical indulgence—a device for containing the demands of the developing world at little trouble and expense" (Alan Keyes, U.S. Ambassador to the UN Economic and Social Committee, 1983).

Challenging UNCTAD-like structures and the confrontational dynamics that prevail in much of the UN system dealing with economic questions is an option. The present bipolar model embodied in much of the UN, simplifying the world into two aggregate rival groups, has no credibility.

Some developing countries have likewise come to realize that some quid pro quo must be offered to the industrialized countries in order to create the parameters for a true, engaging dialogue based on realism rather than moralizing. UNCTAD issues such as commodity stabilization, increased access to developed-country markets, and concessional financial flows appear to be debates of the past. Alister McIntyre, former officer-in-charge at UNCTAD, identified three new areas—trade in services, foreign direct investment, and dialogue on domestic economic policies—as issues where a reformed UNCTAD could help to rekindle a more meaningful North-South dialogue. Meanwhile, accelerated growth in Third World manufacturing and trade is increasingly tied to the forging of relationships among developing countries themselves (South-South trade). This emerging trade phenomenon itself suggests a different economic reality than that which existed in the 1960s or even as recently as a few years ago.

Because of UNCTAD's weak reputation in many circles, its political biases, and its mistaken faith in controlling markets, some have concluded that the organziation needs to be drastically changed. The group system, which has so alienated parties and stalled progress on substantive issues, is also badly in need of alteration. The giant conference (for example, UNCTAD VI), which lasts six weeks and is held every fifth year, could be replaced by smaller, less frequent gatherings. The preparation for these conferences has proven in most instances to be very wasteful. The Belgrade ordeal (UNCTAD VI), in 1983, generated much paper but few agreements. Retreating from its broad range of issues and trying to fashion specific suggestions that are concrete may be a difficult step for UNCTAD, but it is necessary. In the future, UNCTAD will probably have to shrink its role and do a few things better, rather than many things inadequately.

Regardless of radical G–77 demands or wishful thinking, UNCTAD will never be the supreme decisionmaking body within the international economic system. The programs suggested by UNCTAD, the Generalized System of Preference (GSP), Common Fund, Code on Restrictive Business Practices, and certain International Commodity Agreements (ICAs), have been less in fact than those anticipated or originally demanded by the G–77. Working with OECD countries and those developing countries that want to reform the organization, including its secretariat, would take concerted U.S. efforts. Some of these changes could be furthered by bilateral as well as multilateral discussions and pressure, and by something of an orchestrated "counteroffensive" presenting an alternative table of agenda items, with technical studies to substantiate them. This path could work to reform UNCTAD (and, in the process, other UN agencies). It is already clear, however, that UNCTAD is not considered a worthy forum for many international economic discussions. The Committee for Investment and Multinational Enterprises (CIME) at the OECD has, for instance, recently initiated a series of meetings with developing countries on foreign direct investment, and the Development Committee of the World Bank in recent years has become a central forum for discussion of debt issues.

While UNCTAD VI avoided significant adverse effects, little emerged that was positive or useful. The outcome of that conference and of the more recent TDB meetings has underscored the present deadlock in the North-South dialogue, and the utter frustration of many involved. Therefore, some changes are generally assumed to be upcoming, lest the broken record be allowed to continue to play and UNCTAD and other UN agencies slip further into disrepute. The question is how and when will these delinquent UN agencies be brought back to their original, meaningful purposes as designated by their respective charters.

THE FUTURE OF NORTH-SOUTH RELATIONS

The North-South dialogue is not working, mainly because of the ideological insistence upon sterile zero-sum approaches. The outmoded structure, presenting a "we-they" framework, as well as inefficient procedures, prevent any mutually beneficial approaches to international and economic development issues.

Reversing these disturbing trends demands careful attention to the selection of the next secretary general of UNCTAD and UNIDO, and to other senior posts in those bodies. But as mentioned, new and emerging issues could also give the North-South dialogue a more realistic focus in future years. On the other hand, accountability is an issue that has to be resolved immediately. Therefore a UN Joint Inspection Unit (JIU) inspection of UNCTAD is a necessary step in the near future. It appears that the G–77 is less cohesive on its position in UNGA than it is in Geneva. Attempts to merge the unsuccessful NIEO into a vague scheme of global negotiations are going nowhere in New York. So it may be helpful to reconsider at this point more precisely what is and what is not a North-South issue. A studious reconsideration and delimiting of issues could make the dialogue process more realistic by lowering exaggerated expectations that have persisted far too long.

The future of international regulation, one of the hallmarks of UN agencies, is likewise clouded. Whether *economic regulation* aimed at transnational economic activities, shipping or individual commodities; *social regulation* aimed at protecting health, safety, or consumers; or *regulation of access to resources*, such as control of oceans, Antarctica, radio frequencies or the moon—UN activity, from legal treaties to voluntary codes or guidelines, may be on the wane.

International regulations are increasingly viewed as hindrances to business or ploys at supranational centralization. Many international regulations, or attempts at such, appear to have been pushed by the Third World in pursuit of a redistributionist world order, rather than to secure mutual benefits for all nations. With most of the regulatory thrusts of the G–77's NIEO now stalemated, and the regulation of multinational corporations less than successful from the point of view of the Third World, many former critics, in academic circles as well as in the G–77, have changed their minds and are now asking how foreign direct investment can be attracted to the developing countries. The next ten years may witness the completion of codes on such diverse subjects as chemicals, foods, and pharmaceuticals, but the thrust of international regulatory activity has lost much of its former power.

A new realism is slowly but firmly affecting what was an unachievable list of developing country demands. The dialogue has nearly collapsed under the weight of emerging economic realities. Such changes are occurring as

the decline of OPEC countries as net exporters of capital;

the slowing of expansion in official development assistance (ODA);

the selective reduction of private direct investment and bank lending;

the stabilization of oil consumption;

the depressed and weak longer-term prospects for commodity prices;

the success of the NICs and export-led growth; and

the performance of the open, market-led economies and relative failure of planned economies.

These shifts are coalescing to make the present and medium-term economic environment considerably different from that of the time when the NIEO was initially articulated.[3]

The broad, set-piece negotiations, covering a wide variety of objectives embodied in the North-South dialogue, are no longer, if they ever were, productive. The NIEO model for harnessing the international economic system has lost its credibility, even with many Third World stalwarts. Consequently, the future of North-South meetings, in style and substance, needs to shift in the direction of discussions that are of mutual benefit and more concrete. Attention to domestic as well as international issues, and more of a focus on economic growth, with recognition of the increasing differences among the developing countries themselves, are warranted.

If reality is to replace empty rhetoric, future North-South discussions need to be more specific and the negotiations more structured and less open-ended and sermonlike. Expectations have to move from wild demands to achievable measures. The artificial search for global solutions will have to be shunned in order to reach workable solutions to real economic problems affecting interdependent economies. The view that LDCs can be separated and treated outside of the conditions that beset the rest of the world has by now been proven false. Some economists have even doubted that there is a special discipline called "development economics."

What To Do with UNCTAD

One of the reasons for the meager results obtained by UNC-TAD is the theoretical model on which its concept of development rests. Raul Prebisch's center-periphery model has played a major role in the work of many UN organizations—under which the developing countries are condemned to a permanent "underdeveloped" status.

But NIEO advocates today appear to be increasingly confused. Indeed some, including Andre Gunder Frank, have seriously modified their thinking from earlier proclamations and are becoming more skeptical about the reasons for underdevelopment. Unfortunately, too few radicals have considered the possibility that their utopianism is the inevitable result of their own models. Too many important G–77 thinkers function on an abstract ideological plane where neat formulations are offered instead of viable solutions.

Recent academic studies on economic development have produced very different hypotheses from those that appeared in the early 1970s. Today development increasingly is viewed as a process of internal transformation and structural adjustment experienced by individual economies in an effort to achieve objectives such as eradication of poverty and improvements in their standards of living.

This process involves movements within an economy as well as certain ties to the outside. Relationships between different economic sectors, employment, behavior of macroeconomic variables, use of natural resources, the need for imported capital and technology, and many other variables are now considered important. The newer, more dynamic, multidimensional model of economic development that is emerging can be contrasted with the static, center-periphery model that has prevailed in UN G–77 discussions.

UNCTAD could be focused with the UNGA Second (Economic and Social) Committee (ECOSOC) or converted into a small, tighter, specialized agency. At the very least, attempts should be made to force future agendas to avoid duplication. UNCTAD should also be held accountable to General Assembly resolutions. The notion of a ministerial-level TDB meeting in 1986 was avoided altogether. This is fortunate because nothing significant would be negotiated anyway. As a final measure, some U.S. critics have suggested that reduction of the U.S. contribution proportional to its share of UNCTAD's budget be considered as a last-ditch attempt to move the current North-South stalemate off its present course.

Any erosion of the group system would mean that individual nations would have a greater say in pursuit of their own economic interests. G–77 voting strength and political pressure will likely continue into the future. But if the required reforms were somehow achieved, the bloated work programs of all UN agencies could be shrunk, thereby leading to a changed view of the nature and task of UN secretariats with greater overall transparency.

UNCTAD need not be the center of all North-South negotiations. One argument that has been made is to reduce UNCTAD by increasing the use of other, more professional specialized agencies and the Multilateral Development Banks (MDBs). This change might allow the international system to be more responsive to the needs of its members, North and South, alike. Subregional economic groups around the world (EEC, ASEAN, SARC, CELIA) have already bypassed the UN system to bring about greater economic cooperation, including bilateral agreements in investment, technology, and trade questions. Regional economic groupings and trade relationships appear to be the wave of the future and they could prove to be even more important should movement away from the older multilateral UN approaches materialize.

The fear that a refusal by the United States to begin negotiations on the broad range of economic issues raised by the developing countries might trigger a series of unilateral economic and political actions by the South has simply not materialized. The argument that the United States and other consuming countries are presently in a relatively weak bargaining position concerning the oil exporting countries and their emulators in other commodities is empirically wrong. The South's strength in this regard has been widely overestimated. OPEC was a singular case, not a model, and even it is breaking down.

The North-South debate today runs the risk of becoming an anachronism. Global solutions have generally failed to work. With the increasing stratification of the Third World itself, prospects for quick, global solutions appear even more remote. One U.S. commentator summed up the situation well, saying about UNCTAD and the North-South dialogue, "without change—it will become a museum for concepts and assumptions overtaken by time and events, rather than an organization and forum suited to the circumstances of today" (attributed to Richard Kauzlarich, Dep. Asst. Sec. of State for International Organizations, 1983).

The NIEO was unrealistic when it was first proposed and international economic reality has changed even more dramatically since the positions put forward. But international rhetoric has not yet caught up with the new reality. If the South fails to recognize the present state of international economic conditions, the prospects for continued stalemate are high; indeed, the dialogue will earn its rightful place as a low priority item unless it is recast around legitimate, concrete issues that better meet the objectives of all parties concerned.

The U.S. policy of standing firm against the South's sweeping demands has been more or less successful. Indeed the term "South" is itself increasingly amorphous. Many so-called Third World countries are removing themselves from that designation by acting more clearly in their own self-interest. The G–77, which is a disparate collection of countries, totally lacks the cohesion needed to pressure the industrialized countries. It therefore appears that the G–77, to the extent it survives, will only be able to make progress in the North-South arena to the degree it becomes more pragmatic and focuses on economic policies. North-South issues are real but they will have to be recast if they are to be constructively mediated.

NOTES

1. See Karl P. Sauvant, *The Group of 77* (New York: Oceana Publications, Inc., 1981).

2. Development economists are divided on how to categorize the Third World, developing countries. Five stages of progress toward self-sustained growth are, however, clearly observable:

1. Countries grossly deficient in the preconditions for growth, with an annual per-capita income under $300.

2. Countries lacking institutional and other preconditions for sustained growth but with a core of technically trained personnel, adult literacy, considerable infrastructure, import substituting industries, and progress in agricultural output through use of modern technology. Annual per-capita income of less than $700.

3. Countries that have achieved a substantial number of preconditions for growth but require further development assistance to gain self-sustainability. Income per-capita approximately $1,000 a year.

4. Countries that have acquired the capacity for sustained growth with considerable industrialization. A relatively high annual per-capita income of $1,500.

5. Countries with high incomes and rapid growth based wholly on a natural resource, such as oil.

3. See Khadija Haq, *Equality of Opportunity Within and Among Nations* (New York: Praeger, 1977); P.N. Agrawala, *The NIEO: An Overview* (New York: Pergamon, 1984); Henry Jacobson and Dusan Sidanski, *The Emerging International Economic Order* (Santa Barbara: Sage, 1982;) Roger Hansen, *Beyond the North-South Stalemate* (New York: McGraw-Hill, 1979); and Robert Rothstein, *Global Bargaining: UNCTAD and the Quest for a New International Order* (Princeton, N.J.: Princeton University Press, 1979).

9

Foreign Direct Investment Flows to the LDCs

An expanded role of the private sector in developing countries has been a predominant thrust in economic development strategy for less developed countries over the last few years. LDCs themselves have come to realize that they cannot industrialize their economies on a significant scale without the cooperation of developed countries and their associated private sectors (large extraction companies and consortia and multi-national corporations). These transnational economic entities provide access to world markets and marketing systems, control vital technologies, and can call on the managerial and financial resources needed for development and investment.

Many LDCs have come to understand that nationalization and expropriation policies reduce much-needed foreign investment flows. The critical debt situation many developing countries face further requires that financing for projects come from developed countries, and particularly their private sectors and not via LDC borrowing. The LDCs that have made the greatest strides toward self-sustaining growth have been those who relied to the greatest extent on market forces in their own economies. The expertise and capital of the U.S. private sector has and can foster and enhance the indigenous private sectors of many developing countries. Moreover, it has been proven that policies that are pursued by LDCs to attract foreign investment facilitate domestic capital formation. Indigenous capital investment is the key to sustained economic development.

Direct international investment, foreign direct investment

(FDI), or private investment—all the same—takes place in response to perceived profit opportunities. With the exception of purchases of real assets by individuals, direct investment has been primarily a corporate phenomenon. Direct investment occurs when a corporation establishes a foreign subsidiary firm or when a parent corporation buys out resident minority stockholders of a foreign subsidiary or a joint venture is broached.[1]

When a nation runs a surplus on its trade account that is matched by an investment outflow, the pattern of foreign demand reflects the expenditures made with the investment funds. Acquisition of assets in a foreign country involves setting up a foreign subsidiary (extractive, sales, or manufacturing) and generally requires the importation of capital goods.

MULTINATIONAL CORPORATIONS

The existence of multinational corporations (MNCs) facilitates movement of capital and technology among nations. Industry-specific factors are generally the factors that move most quickly to respond to profitable opportunities. These movements improve the efficiency of global resource allocation. An MNCs ability to assemble industry specific factors in functional groupings, that include human capital, is far greater than would be possible in a system of decentralized markets. This ability applies to trade in commodities as well, because these companies possess better knowledge of trading advantages and communications.

MNC organizational forms allow them to operate in a realm beyond nationalism so as to increase the global product. The contact between operatives at the supranational level (MNCs) and the national level (government and citizens) can however cause some friction. MNCs generally invest abroad to enlarge markets, so as to increase their profits. By doing so MNCs tend to expose their investments to both political and economic risks. There are at least three ways to reduce these risks: (1) careful selection of host countries; (2) prearrangements or concessions concerning treatment of the subsidiary; and (3) creation of a joint venture by buying into an ongoing corporation or endowing a subsidiary with a significant amount of host country national ownership.

The direct investment decisions of MNCs respond to different anticipated yields (rates of return) in specific industries and, therefore, are usually tied to investment by an MNC to an industry in which it already has or foresees gaining a competitive advantage. These flows tend to be highly industry-specific, and rely heavily on nongeneric factors of production as a source of motivation. Some of the primary reasons for direct investment on the part of large firms include

overall investment plans;

protection of existing markets;

search for lower cost production;

diversification;

profitability of overseas markets; and

receptive attitudes and policies of LDCs.

The manufacturing sector has generally been regarded as best suited to FDI, with durable goods most favorable. Geographically, broad trends in private investment are observable. Asian NICs are now rated most highly while Latin American NICs are falling in the proportion of FDI they receive. Numerous elements tend to influence FDI decisions including:

access to domestic or regional or markets;

avoidance of tariff and nontariff barriers;

changes in industry structure;

slow growth in home markets;

availability of raw materials;

inducements from host governments;

comparative labor and material costs;

political and social stability;

tax advantages;

return on investment;

acquisition opportunities; and

exchange rate movements.

MEASURING FLOWS OF DIRECT INVESTMENT

Flows of direct investment are relatively insensitive to changes either in product development or in interest rates. In the short run, outflows of direct investment tend to be dominated by changes in market conditions abroad, changes in market structure, and technological developments. Given that these influences are only remotely connected to the instrument variables of international payments policy, international saving has to adjust to international investment. Current accounts are subject to year-to-year variation if the flow out is uneven and if basic balance is to be achieved. Rates of exchange may have to change frequently as direct investment can cause balance-of-payments strains under a system of fixed exchange rates, in turn causing target rates of domestic economic performance to be lowered.

Developed-country investment in LDCs is virtually all private direct investment. (See Table 9.1.) FDI increased rapidly in oil-importing LDCs in the 1960s and early 1970s but did not continue in the late 1970s or 1980s. The United States presently accounts for approximately 48 percent of the world's foreign direct investment. Most of the remainder comes from Western Europe,

Table 9.1
NET FDI FLOWS, 1975–82
($ Billion)

Year	U.S.	W. Eur.	Japan	LDCs
1975	−11.6	−0.9	−1.5	+5.3
1976	−7.3	−4.4	−1.9	+5.0
1977	−7.9	−2.0	−1.6	+5.4
1978	−8.5	−3.4	−2.4	+7.3
1979	−14.6	−8.3	−2.9	+8.9
1980	−5.6	−6.7	−2.1	+10.1
1981	+12.6	−24.0	−4.7	+13.9
1982	+12.2	−13.0	−4.9	+11.4

Source: UN Center for Transnational Corporations.

Japan, and Canada. Since 1982, U.S. parent companies no longer undertook a majority of the direct investment. Increasingly Third World countries such as Argentina, Brazil, Colombia, Hong Kong, India, Peru, South Korea, Singapore, Taiwan, the Philippines, and the OPEC countries have themselves started establishing MNCs.

Many LDC governments have been ambivalent about, even hostile to, direct foreign investment and to the MNCs involved therein. Some governments fear a loss of sovereignty and have come to distrust MNCs or have impeded creation of an open climate for investment.

Third World leaders are generally ambivalent on the subject of U.S. private direct investment. Some want more FDI and local entrepreneurship, while others castigate the role of foreign capital and the very nature of MNCs.

LDC attitudes and policies toward FDI tend to fall into three broad categories:

1. Opposition—those viewing the multinationals as evil. Nationalization and expropriation are considered legitimate. Marxist and nationalist ideologies promulgate the control of foreign/capitalist influences, for example, Ethiopia, Guyana, and other radical states.

2. Pragmatism—FDI is viewed with mixed feelings. Private sectors are not disallowed but negotiated entry can range from difficult and bureaucratic to relatively simple and forthright, that is, Nigeria and most Latin American countries.

3. Advocation—Increasingly many LDC leaders have witnessed the positive benefits of FDI, as partners in development. Open-door policies in these countries encourage private-sector activity and grant more or less unrestricted entry, for example, Jamaica, Asian NICs, and Malawi.

According to one account, total sales in 1982 of the largest 33 MNCs with branches in the Third World exceeded $90 billion. Large MNCs with hundreds of branches throughout the world can have an output comparable to LDCs with which they bargain. UNCTAD estimated that MNC production in the early 1980s accounted for 20 percent of world output and that intrafirm trade stood at 25 percent of international manufacturing trade. The markets MNCs operate in are often oligopolistic with competition among few sellers whose pricing policies are interdependent if not vertically integrated.

But overall, the United States has argued that multinationals can help developing countries to

finance balance-of-payment deficits;

acquire specialized goods and services;

obtain technology to increase productivity;

provide management and entrepreneurship;

make contacts with overseas banks, markets, and suppliers;

train domestic technicians;

employ domestic labor;

generate tax revenue;

increase national income by specialization and economies of scale; and

enhance efficiency, including world trade.

The World Bank's Development Report for 1983 stated, "The outlook for foreign direct investment has become more attractive recently, since the cost of borrowing has risen and an understanding has been reached between investors and some host governments." With the prospects for bank lending more constrained, direct investment may contribute a greater share of the capital flows to developing countries. However, the scope for substitution is limited to the private sector; direct investment cannot be used to finance most development infrastructure.

The redeployment of some less competitive industries to developing countries has tended to be concentrated in a limited number of countries—South Korea, Taiwan, Singapore, Brazil, and Mexico. Developed countries have to date placed few restrictions on foreign investments of their companies. However most LDCs still enforce industrial policies limiting MNCs to a level and conduct consistent with prescribed local interests. These limits vary widely according to country.

Official data compiled by the World Bank, the Development Assistance Committee (DAC) of the OECD, and the UN Center on Transnational Corporations[2] has estimated direct investment flows worldwide, but these organizations have difficulty col-

Table 9.2
Total Net Resource Receipts of LDCs from All Sources
Current Prices ($ Billion)

	1970	1975	1980	1981	1982
Official development assistance	8.23	20.95	37.33	36.63	34.24
Grants by private voluntary agencies	0.86	1.34	2.31	2.02	2.31
Nonconcessional flows	10.95	34.31	56.41	69.27	56.63
Private	6.99	23.78	33.92	47.13	34.00
A) Direct	3.69	11.36	10.54	16.13	11.00
B) Bank	3.00	12.00	22.00	29.00	21.00
C) Bond lending	0.30	0.42	1.38	2.00	2.00
Total receipts	20.04	56.60	96.05	107.92	93.18

Source: Organization for Economic Cooperation and Development.

lecting and reconciling information from the large number of countries. Unfortunately most of their data are 18 months out of date. A Group of Thirty study, "Foreign Direct Investment 1973–87," showed that during the last 20 years, an average of 35 percent of total international direct investment flows went to the developing countries. FDI flows declined from 60 percent to only 20 percent of net private flows to LDCs in the same time period. (See Table 9.2.) The World Bank has however projected a rise by as much as 40 percent of private flows by 1995. An important aspect of the flows to developing countries, even though relatively small in terms of the total flow, is that they often represent

Table 9.3
Developed Country Investment Flows

DAC Country	Share in Investment Flow		Average Annual Growth Rate
	1970–72	1979–82	
Australia	2.3	1.1	5
Austria	0	0.2	25
Belgium	1.2	1.6	18
Canada	2.8	2.7	14
Denmark	0.4	0.6	19
Finland	0	0.2	76
France	5.7	7.3	18
Germany	11.4	10.1	13
Italy	5.5	2.4	4
Japan	6.1	10.9	22
Netherlands	5.6	1.8	0
New Zealand	0	0.1	NA
Norway	0.3	0.1	–4
Sweden	1.1	0.8	11
Switzerland	1.7	3.0	21
United Kingdom	8.6	8.9	15
United States	47.3	48.2	14
Total	100.0	100.0	14

Source: Organization for Economic Cooperation and Development.

Table 9.4
Geographical Distribution of Private Direct Investment from OPEC and DAC Countries to LDCs in 1982 (millions of dollars)

Afghanistan	0.1	Guinea-Bissau	—
Algeria	−116.7	Guyana	0
Angola	118.8	Haiti	−0.3
Argentina	380.9	Honduras	−0.3
Bahamas	335.9	Hong Kong	527.8
Bangladesh	1.0	India	34.1
Barbados	0.3	Indonesia	530.4
Belize	−2.0	Iran	−131.1
Benin	0.1	Iraq	2.4
Bermuda	1,046.0	Israel	66.2
Bolivia	0.5	Ivory Coast	58.0
Botswana	0.9	Jamaica	6.2
Brazil	1,388.8	Jordan	0.1
Burma	—	Kampuchea	—
Burundi	0.9	Kenya	1.8
Cameroon	43.5	Kiribati	—
Central Afr. Rep.	1.1	Korea, Republic of	108.3
Chad	—	Laos	—
Chile	18.8	Lebanon	0.3
China	41.6	Lesotho	—
Colombia	509.0	Liberia	313.9
Comoros	0.2	Madagasgar	−0.1
Congo	15.4	Malawi	—
Costa Rica	0.1	Malaysia	260.3
Cuba	0	Mali	2.8
Cyprus	−16.9	Mauritania	−1.1
Djibouti	−0.1	Mauritus	0.2
Dominican Republic	0	Mexico	−1,039.5
Ecuador	129.3	Morocco	9.3
Egypt	305.2	Mozambique	1.9
El Salvador	−2.6	Nepal	0
Ethiopia	0	Nicaragua	—
Fiji	5.4	Niger	−2.1
Gabon	102.6	Nigeria	389.6
Gambia	0.3	Pakistan	−0.7
Ghana	—	Panama	1,090.8
Greece	−21.9	Papua New Guinea	84.5
Guatemala	81.2	Paraguay	14.6
Guinea	—	Peru	373.8

Table 9.4—*Continued*

Philippines	123.6	Togo	0.2
Portugal	178.0	Trinidad and Tobago	24.0
Rwanda	1.4	Tunisia	21.9
Senegal	4.5	Turkey	−61.7
Seychelles	0	Uganda	0
Sierra Leone	−0.1	Upper Volta	−0.2
Singapore	192.4	Uruguay	0.7
Somalia	55.8	Vanuatu	7.6
Sri Lanka	3.2	Viet Nam	13.1
Sudan	16.8	Western Samoa	—
Surinam	0	Yemen	51.8
Swaziland	—	Yemen, Dem.	—
Syria	—	Yugoslavia	0.3
Taiwan	59.1	Zaire	−7.4
Tanzania	14.3	Zambia	21.4
Thailand	127.9	Zimbabwe	−0.7
		Total	11,857.9

Source: Organization for Economic Cooperation and Development.

large inflows for the individual host countries involved. According to the DAC, direct investment inflows from developed countries to developing countries rose fourfold over 11 years to more than $15.5 billion in 1981 in nominal terms, an increase of 55 percent in real terms. (See Tables 9.3 and 9.4.) Some disinvestment, notably in Latin America, has also occurred.

According to the World Bank studies, FDI could grow by as much as 9.2 percent per year in the 1982–95 period after experiencing negative growth of −0.4 percent during 1980–82. Bank lending over the last 15 years has probably substituted for foreign investment, given the low interest rates operative through the 1970s and various restrictions on MNC investments. The overall outlook for FDI is looking much better now that the cost of borrowing has risen and host governments are more receptive. Constrained bank lending means FDI will contribute a greater share of the capital flows to developing countries in the near future. Foreign investment cannot, however, be directly interchanged with bank lending, as private investments tend to be limited to certain sectors in the economy.

NOTES

1. Outward direct investment by U.S. residents is free. The United States participates in 114 bilateral investment agreements with LDCs, which provide procedurally for the operations of the U.S. Overseas Private Investment Corporation (OPIC), established in 1971 to conduct financing, insurance, and reinsurance operations. OPIC's Investment Insurance Program offers investors protection against loss due to political risks. A Bureau for Private Enterprise (PRE) was established within the Agency for International Development (AID) to promote economic growth and development through stimulation and expansion of private, small, indigenous business enterprises. The bureau focuses on 12 selected countries and the Caribbean Basin. Other official U.S. support to private direct investment comes from: the International Executive Service Corps (IESC), a nonprofit, private group of U.S. businessmen who provide technical skills to LDCs; volunteers in International Technical Assistance (VITA), a private, nonprofit corporation that assists (through correspondence) small businesses in developing countries; and Partners of the Alliance, a business link for entrepreneurs in Latin America.

2. UN responses to MNCs have been wide-ranging and far-reaching. Five of the six principal bodies and eighteen of the fifty-two related agencies in the UN system have taken up activities of concern in MNCs. Efforts have been fragmented or highly specific depending on the mandate of the particular bodies in the system. The UNGA has focused on foreign direct investment since the onset of the North-South debate in the late 1960s. The NIEO set out proposals for trade, commodities, the monetary system, cooperation, industrialization, and technology transfer that demand the strict regulation of MNCs. UNCTAD, founded in 1964, was designed to help developing nations expand trade: at the 23rd Pugwash Conference on Science and World Affairs UNCTAD was called on to set up a working group for a Code of Conduct on the Transfer of Technology. UNIDO, founded in 1967, has sought to provide technical assistance to developing countries and to coordinate the policies of developed nations in that process. It has helped facilitate foreign direct investment and to publicize investment opportunities. The ILO, organized in 1919 and maintained as a specialized UN agency in 1946, has initiated a series of studies dealing with employment implications of MNC activities. ECOSOC's involvement with MNC issues dates from 1972, when developing countries accused MNCs of political interference. The UN Center on TNCs and Commission on TNCs have worked on a code of conduct and collected information on MNC behavior since 1975.

10

LDC Criticism of the Pharmaceutical Industry in UN Forums

In the World Health Organization (WHO) and other UN agencies, less developed country (LDC) spokespersons have voiced growing concern over what they regard as unfair pricing, inadequate quality control, and various unethical practices by the multinational drug companies.[1] UN bodies have discussed such topics as measures to guarantee drug quality, facilitate drug production in developing countries, and concentrate LDC purchases on essential drugs. Some of these would extend the sort of regulation commonly found in developed countries. Other proposals seem antibusiness in nature and economically unsound.

Developing countries depend heavily on imports for pharmaceuticals, mainly because of their own technological weakness. To date only a few LDCs have established advanced production capabilities for the manufacture of pharmaceuticals. Some others engage in the final manufacturing stages of dosage formulation and packaging.

Annual pharmaceutical[2] expenditures in developing countries total $15–20 billion, between one-third and one-half of health expenditures, compared with developed-country drug outlays exceeding $100 billion, one-sixth of health expenditures. Sales to LDCs of pharmaceuticals amount to 23 percent of international pharmaceutical trade. Annual spending per person on pharmaceuticals is estimated at $15 in Mexico, $12 in Brazil, $16 in Nigeria, and $1 in India, compared with more than $100 in Western Europe, Japan and the United States. Annual pharmaceutical sales in the Third World are projected by a private industry source to double within the next two decades.

Developing countries depend on imports for more than 50 percent of their apparent consumption of pharmaceuticals.[3] Drug companies have been reluctant to manufacture in LDCs, pointing to a lack of skilled labor and high startup costs, the sophisticated technology required, and the relatively low cost of shipping drugs long distances. In 1982 the two largest producers in the global pharmaceutical market were the United States, 21.3 percent, and Japan, 15.1 percent. Pharmaceutical research and development are concentrated in the developed countries, and the heaviest investment in the industry continues to take place in the United States and Japan.

For years, developing countries have sought relief through the United Nations for abuses they contend that they suffer from multinational drug companies. LDC critics of the pharmaceutical industry have alleged that the market power of the multinational companies allows them to engage in excessive and even abusive pricing, exaggerated promotional and marketing efforts, dissemination of faulty information, wasteful proliferation of brand names and products, and use of patents as entry barriers—while they perform insufficient research on Third World diseases. Some have argued that pharmaceuticals should be sold to LDCs at marginal cost.

Where competition is weak, charges indeed have been high. The antituberculosis drug isonazid has sold for 10 times more in Niger than in Nigeria, the antibiotic streptomycin 12 times more in Guinea than in Egypt. On average, however, developing countries do not pay more than other countries for the drugs they buy, at least according to a study conducted by one U.S. economist.[4] Moreover, the argument that pharmaceuticals should be made available to LDCs at marginal cost overlooks the cost of research and development for past and future pharmaceutical production.

RELIEF SOUGHT BY LDCs

A wide variety of solutions has been suggested to problems related to pharmaceutical production. Many studies on pharmaceutical-related questions have been undertaken since the mid–1970s by WHO and other UN organizations.[5] Together these initiatives have constituted a plea for what is dubbed a New International Pharmaceutical Order.

LDCs have tried to lessen their "exploitation" at the hands of the multinational drug companies by getting UN agencies to

improve quality control by either requiring exporting governments to guarantee quality, or instituting international regulation;

facilitate a shift in production to the LDCs by abolishing patents and encouraging technology transfer;

help LDCs limit imports to "needed" drugs;

foster LDC group-purchase arrangements; and

regulate labeling and marketing practices.

Developing countries could take some of these steps on their own, as many developed countries have. In the United Nations they tend to politicize pharmaceutical issues and treat them as an extension of the North-South dialogue.

Quality Control

Certification schemes would require appropriate governmental agencies (such as the ministries of health in exporting countries) to certify to importing countries that products were approved for marketing. Certification has been voluntarily adopted by many industrialized countries but has not gained wide support in developing countries. Numerous UN agencies have recommended that no drug be sold internationally until approved for use where it was initially manufactured. Developed countries require investigational procedures or preclinical trials, proof of safety and efficacy, and accurate labeling. In the United States, for example, Food and Drug Administration approval requires elaborate animal and clinical testing of all new drugs. The United Kingdom also has tight controls requiring proof of efficacy. Japan has strict premarket clearance procedures. Some countries where drugs are developed or manufactured are much less demanding, however, and companies wishing to evade certification or country-of-origin rules could do so by moving research and production of drugs to countries where marketing approval could be obtained easily.

WHO has set some standards for marketing and provides information to national governments, but some of the least developed countries lack the administrative and legal establishments to take full advantage of the program. Proposals have been made to mandate WHO as an international tester of drugs to establish standards for worldwide guidance. WHO, however, has not sought this responsibility, and the proposals have languished.

Local Production, Technology Transfer, and Patents

One long-term solution to the exploitation problem would be for LDCs to produce and distribute pharmaceutical products themselves. Some radical advocates have called for the abolition of all or most drug patents to facilitate the transfer of drug technology. This measure, however, could discourage industrial research and development. A few LDCs already have ignored international patents, and industrial nations increasingly have encouraged licensing, and in some cases have even implemented compulsory licensing after an initial period of monopoly. Few of the essential drugs on the WHO list are still covered by patents.

In any event, both profit/loss accounting and social cost/benefit analysis according to UNIDO guidelines or other methodologies probably would rule against attempts to inaugurate pharmaceutical industries in most LDCs. In the early years, the capital cost—most of it in foreign exchange—would be very high. The best prospects would be in the most populous LDCs, which have very large potential markets, and in a few of the newly industrializing countries, which might be able to achieve comparative advantage in bulk drug production and become substantial exporters. Important local drug industries to date have been developed in only four LDCs—Mexico, Brazil, India, and Cuba. China, Egypt, and Argentina have made substantial progress in the development of local manufacture of pharmaceuticals.

Producing finished chemicals from raw materials requires complex and expensive equipment, sophisticated technical knowledge, and skilled workers. For LDCs, this means extensive investment and technology transfer. And in the end, innovation is most likely to occur in large-scale laboratories working under competitive pressures. The U.S. Pharmaceutical Manufacturers Association (PMA) estimates the cost per approved new single-entity drug at $54 million. Research time typically is several years. No drug classified as "essential" by the United Nations has yet been developed in the Third World.[6]

National Formularies

Some LDCs have published formularies, that is, listings of those drugs recommended for particular uses, to curb what they regard as undesirable proliferation of drugs. Sri Lanka, for instance, has a formulary with only a few hundred items. India's basic drug needs have been estimated by the government at 116 generic drugs, less than 1 percent of the 15,000 branded drugs sold there. Bangladesh since 1982 has pursued a New Drug Policy which embodies the formulary approach. As long ago as 1977, WHO published its list of essential drugs totaling 214 products; 182 were classified as "essential" and 32 as "complementary." The list is only suggestive and has no force of law.

The stated objective of the formulary approach is not to reduce total drug expenditures (which generally are agreed to be inadequate in Third World countries) but to concentrate expenditures to provide the greatest benefits to the most patients. Drug companies appear increasingly willing to accept this approach as long as formularies cover only government purchases of drugs.

Group Purchase

The purchase of large quantities of drugs to qualify for discounts on the basis of competitive bids is a proven technique that LDCs can use to reduce the cost of generic drugs. Group-purchase schemes can be used within a single nation or by several small countries through an international agency. The 12 nations (population 15 million) in the Caribbean Community (CARICOM) recently tried to start a group-purchase scheme to meet their pharmaceutical needs. Group purchases have been considered by the Association of Southeast Asian Nations (ASEAN) since at least 1980. The islands of the South Pacific have also initiated a subregional center for procurement of pharmaceuticals, and separate groups of East and West African nations are exploring the possibilities for bulk purchases. UNICEF buys its drugs in bulk but does not appear willing to become a drug-purchasing agent for the Third World.

Labeling and Marketing

Inaccurate drug labeling has been cited by LDCs and consumer groups as a major problem area. The critics do not demand uniform labeling worldwide, because nutrition, climate, and other factors clearly vary from region to region and can affect dosage, storage, and proper use. The PMA has adopted a resolution on international labeling of prescription medicine which has brought some improvement in labeling. The International Federation of Pharmaceutical Manufacturer's Associations has also enacted a code of pharmaceutical marketing procedures to support ethical principles and voluntary practices in keeping with the industry's international responsibilities. These codes have quelled neither demands for stronger measures nor harsh criticism of the marketing procedures of the large corporations producing drugs. However, the PMA has won kudos for its role in an innovative pilot program for distributing pharmaceuticals in Gambia.

UN agencies have suggested devising an internationally recognized guideline for good promotional practices. Some of the major pharmaceutical firms, sensing growing support for a mandatory marketing code, have talked about pushing such alternative approaches as creation of an ombudsmanlike office to monitor the industry's own code.

ROLES OF UN AGENCIES TO DATE

Contentious deliberations over pharmaceutical practices,[7] trade,[8] and transfer of technology[9] have taken place as the UN system has given increased priority to a myriad of pharmaceutical issues over the last two decades. Protracted discussions have not solved and are not likely to solve many of these issues.

Two nongovernmental consumer organizations, and on occasion the Nordic countries, have been active on the LDC side of pharmaceutical issues in UN bodies. Health Action International (HAI), established in 1981, has promoted full implementation of programs on essential drugs and in certain instances has supported LDCs with both technical expertise and argumentation. The International Organization of Consumers Unions (IOCU), founded in 1960, has coordinated its network of consumer groups to advocate positions on pharmaceuticals. Individual authors also have condemned the pharmaceutical multinationals and offered suggestions.[10]

The major UN agencies involved in pharmaceutical issues are WHO, UNCTAD, UNIDO, UNITAR, and UNCTC. The most prominent and highly qualified among the UN organizations dealing with pharmaceutical matters is WHO.

Since 1962 WHO has been given the responsibility to

establish minimum basic requirements and recommend standard methods for the chemical and pharmacological evaluation of pharmaceutical preparations;

ensure a regular exchange of information on the safety and efficacy of pharmaceutical preparations; and

secure prompt transmission to national health authorities of new information on serious side effects of pharmaceutical preparations.

Over the years WHO has issued scientific reports on the general principles of toxicological testing of drugs (assessing bioavailability, mutagenicity, and carcinogenicity) and has developed an international scheme for monitoring adverse drug reactions. Its international drug monitoring system is now more than 10 years old, and the number of participating countries exceeds 25. Other WHO achievements are listed below.

A data base of more than 200,000 items is being augmented at a rate of 4,000 entries per month.

The WHO "Certification Scheme on the Quality of Pharmaceutical Products Moving in International Commerce," adopted in 1975, now includes 107 countries and has enlisted the cooperation of the International Federation of Manufacturers Associations.

Some 114 national information offices currently receive monthly information from WHO detailing restrictive drug regulatory decisions.

The Third International Conference of Drug Regulatory Authorities was held in Stockholm June 11–14, 1984.

The WHO *Drug Information Bulletin* provides edited commentary on national decisions.

WHO's *International Digest of Health Legislation* regularly publishes texts of national laws, and the WHO *International Pharmacopoeia* contains descriptions of general methods of analysis, including individual quality specifications for drugs widely used in healthcare.

Other UN agencies have carved out niches for themselves in the pharmaceutical field, but little has been done to coordinate activities under way within the UN system. The UNCTAD Secretariat has tried to take a lead role, but it has not met with much success.[11]

UNCTAD members continue to promote initiatives on trademarks, consumer protection, generic drugs, and technology transfer. They once again considered pharmaceutical issues at the 29th Trade and Development Board meeting in September 1984 and in various sessions thereafter. UNIDO has been concerned with contractual arrangements for the production of drugs, facilitation of processing in LDCs, trade issues, and questions related to patents. UNITAR has studied technology transfer in the pharmaceutical industry in some detail but in recent years has reported little on these topics. UNCTC is interested in the proposed code governing multinational corporations. It has regarded the pharmaceutical industry as a case study on the need for strong regulatory measures against them.

Wrangling over pharmaceutical issues is likely to continue in UN forums even if the pharmaceutical industry redoubles its efforts to provide quality drugs at affordable prices. LDCs, joined sometimes by the Nordic countries, will press for a combination of measures designed to bring about a New International Pharmaceutical Order, while the multinational drug companies will resist additional controls and any UN programs aimed at promoting pharmaceutical production by state agencies in LDCs. The multinational companies are likely to continue advocating self-policing to head off tighter statutory regulation. They will argue that increased regulation would discourage investment in and production and distribution of needed medicines. In the absence of a major tightening of statutory regulation, the LDCs no doubt will continue to make allegations of overpricing and unethical practices.

The drug companies argue with considerable justification that proposals currently under scrutiny in most UN agencies, if implemented, would give ill-equipped, ill-staffed governmental agencies tasks that the private sector could perform more reliably and effectively. Moreover, if LDCs actually followed all or even most of the policies advocated in proposed guidelines, they might be unable to attract foreign direct investment by private pharmaceutical companies.

A positive development would be the emergence of WHO as the unquestioned leader in broad areas of international pharmaceutical oversight. Conceivably, WHO could become the focal point for all international pharmaceutical issues. This trend is unlikely to mature, however, because other UN agencies probably will continue to politicize these matters and seek to enlarge their respective mandates.

NOTES

1. Pharmaceutical issues have been circulating in various UN forums since the mid–1960s. The fourth session of the UN Conference on Trade and Development (UNCTAD) in 1976 called for cooperation among developing countries on pharmaceuticals. The fifth conference of the nonaligned movement (NAM) in 1978 adopted a resolution calling for comprehensive action. The Economic Cooperation among Developing Countries (ECDC) conference of the G–77 endorsed these moves, and in 1977 a UN task force on pharmaceuticals was established. The sixth NAM conference in 1979 endorsed specific recommendations and called, among other things, for the establishment within 2 years of 3–6 regional cooperative pharmaceutical production and technology centers and 3–6 formulation plants in the developing countries.

2. Pharmaceutical products are those drugs administered by per-

sons trained in pharmacy and include all medicinal drugs sold over the counter and by prescription.

3. Some LDCs, recognizing this fact, have issued or intend to issue directives to promote self-sufficiency in pharmaceuticals. Mexico recently revised its regulations to ensure that all of the 30 drugs officially designated most basic will be produced domestically within five years. The Mexican government supports research and development that leads to local production, encourages mergers of small companies, provides low-cost loans to companies with at least 51 percent Mexican ownership, and protects producers of raw chemicals.

4. John E. S. Parker, "Pharmaceuticals and Third World Concerns," *The International Supply of Medicines*, ed. Robert B. Helms (Washington, D.C.: American Enterprise Institute, 1980).

5. UNCTAD, the UN Industrial Development Organization (UNIDO), the UN Children's Fund (UNICEF), the UN Development Program (UNDP), the UN Centre on Transnational Corporations (UNCTC), and the UN Institute for Training and Research (UNITAR).

6. Yesterday's drugs were products of serendipity. Today's depend on design and research with clear medical objectives. The drug discoveries of 1890–1970 (aspirin, sulphonamonides, antibiotics, antihypertensives, tranquilizers, antiarthritics, and beta-blockers) were based on tissue biochemistry. Drugs developed since 1970 (antivirals, cancer therapy, and treatments for autoimmune diseases) have been based on cell biochemistry.

7. See UNIDO, "Contractual Arrangements for the Production of Drugs," 1983; UNCTAD, "The Role of Trademarks in the Promotion of Exports from Developing Countries," 1982; UNCTAD, "Trademarks and Generic Names of Pharmaceuticals and Consumer Production," 1982; and WHO, "Policies for the Production and Marketing of Essential Drugs," 1983.

8. See UNCTC, "Transnational Corporations and the Pharmaceutical Industry," 1979; UNCTAD, "Guidelines on Technology Issues in the Pharmaceutical Sector in the Developing Countries," 1982; and UNIDO, "Pharmaceuticals in the Developing World: Policies on Drugs, Trade, and Production," 1979.

9. See UNIDO, "Second Consultation on the Pharmaceutical Industry," 1983; UNITAR "Technology Transfer in the Pharmaceutical Industry," 1971; UNCTAD, "Technology Policies and Planning for the Pharmaceutical Sector in the Developing Countries," 1980; UNCTAD, "Major Issues in the Transfer of Technology to Developing Countries: A Case Study of the Pharmaceutical Industry," 1975; and UNIDO, "Sum-

mary of the Industrial Property Protection on Pharmaceuticals in Developing Countries," 1979.

10. See, for example, Milton Silverman et al., *Prescriptions for Death: The Drugging of the Third World* (Berkeley: University of California Press, 1982). The same author has published *Pills, Profits, and Politics* and *Drugging of the Americas*; Diana Melrose, *The Great Health Robbery* (Oxford: Oxfam, 1981). The same author has published *Bitter Pills* (Oxford: Oxfam, 1983); T. Heller, *Poor Health, Rich Profits.* (Nottingham, England: Spokesman Books, 1977); Charles Meadawar, *Drug Disinformation* (London: Social Audit, 1980); Virginia Beardshaw, *Prescription for Change* (London: HAI, 1982).

11. See UNCTAD, "Guidelines on Technology Issues in the Pharmaceutical Sector in Developing Countries," 1982.

11

South-South Trade: A Growing Phenomenon

One of the chief ways developing countries are trying to increase economic cooperation and development is by expanding their mutual trade. The importance of trade among the developing countries, or so-called South-South trade, has been enhanced by the slowed growth in world trade and the recent global recession. During the 1970s the exports of developing countries grew faster than the exports of the rest of the world. Even in the 1980s with the growth of developing country exports to the world declining by 3 percent, intra-LDC exports continued to rise by more than 4 percent. The share of developing countries in world trade has increased in the last two decades from under 20 percent to over 28 percent. This growth benefits not only individual developing countries but also, by lowering import penetration, effects the developed economies such as the United States.

While exports from Asia account for the greatest share of inter-LDC trade, African and Latin American trade has grown in spite of the high degree of protectionism in many LDC markets. (See Table 11.1.) Trade in fuel is by far the largest single category, followed by food. Manufacturing-sector trade accounts for over $2 billion worth of total South-South trade, with Asian manufacturing outstripping other LDC exports in the manufacturing area by two to one, giving further evidence of the East Asian newly industrialized country (NIC) phenomenon. Because of the general level of economic development, African exports are far smaller and regional in nature of destination than the exports of other LDCs. (See Table 11.2.)

Table 11.1
Network of Intra-trade and Inter-trade of Developing Countries, 1982

Exports from	Exports to				
	Americas	Africa	West Asia	S. & S.E. Asia	Developing Countries ($ million)
	Percentage				
All Commodities					
Americas	81.7	7.9	3.9	6.5	27,696
Africa	37.3	23.6	27.7	11.2	8,476
West Asia	17.1	8.1	28.3	46.5	49,392
South and Southeast Asia	9.6	8.9	14.9	65.2	52,105
Fuels					
Americas	84.0	8.5	2.4	5.0	15,156
Africa	63.2	15.6	17.9	3.4	6,257
West Asia	21.2	6.8	19.2	52.9	49,251
South and Southeast Asia	7.9	0.4	3.1	85.4	12,056
Food					
Americas	49.9	19.8	22.3	8.0	4,079
Africa	17.9	38.6	30.2	13.4	1,635
West Asia	1.0	10.6	85.0	3.5	2,046
South and Southeast Asia	2.2	13.0	27.4	55.4	5,946
Agricultural raw materials and fertilizers					
Americas	63.1	3.6	9.7	23.5	672
Africa	28.3	34.5	5.2	31.7	385
West Asia	0.3	27.4	66.7	5.3	303
South and Southeast Asia	9.2	5.3	7.6	76.0	3,378
Chemical products					
Americas	83.7	2.3	7.3	6.7	1,587
Africa	1.8	28.9	20.4	48.9	450
West Asia	1.6	8.8	51.8	37.9	672
South and Southeast Asia	4.9	7.1	7.0	80.5	2,043

Table 11.1—**Continued**

Exports from	Exports to				
	Americas	Africa	West Asia	S. & S.E. Asia	Developing Countries ($ million)
	Percentage				
Steel, iron and nonferrous metals					
Americas	66.4	4.	7.2	22.2	1,115
Africa	11.0	27.0	6.5	56.0	200
West Asia	0.8	10.0	82.9	6.6	381
South and Southeast Asia	2.9	3.7	24.6	68.4	2,017
Machinery and transport equipment					
Americas	69.2	15.7	7.5	7.6	2,618
Africa	4.2	85.2	9.9	0.7	142
West Asia	0.1	9.2	82.7	8.0	2,292
South and Southeast Asia	8.8	15.0	10.0	65.9	8,516
Other manufactures					
Americas	79.7	8.4	6.3	5.6	6,897
Africa	4.8	53.2	16.9	25.2	1,174
West Asia	0.2	10.6	81.7	7.5	6,509
South and Southeast Asia	8.0	11.0	20.7	59.0	24,734
Total manufactures					
Americas	87.7	4.9	4.5	3.0	2,692
Africa	7.2	64.1	15.8	12.9	582
West Asia	0.1	11.8	86.6	1.4	3,545
South and Southeast Asia	8.0	10.1	29.1	51.8	14,175

Source: United Nations Conference on Trade and Development.

Table 11.2
Developing Country Trade by Region and by Product Group (Percentage)

Commodity / Exports from	Year	Total exports (less fuels)	Food	Agricultural raw materials and fertilizers	Chemical products	Steel, iron and nonferrous metals	Machinery and transport equipment	Other manufactures	Total manufactures
Americas	1960	100	64.6	18.2	3.5	4.4	1.4	7.0	11.9
	1981	100	32.8	8.2	10.0	6.3	21.4	20.8	52.2
Africa	1960	100	52.4	24.4	3.0	6.5	1.6	10.4	15.0
	1981	100	45.4	16.3	12.9	5.3	4.0	16.1	33.1
West Asia	1960	100	38.5	16.0	2.0	—	5.0	31.0	38.0
	1981	100	24.2	7.0	7.3	—	21.7	39.4	68.1
South and Southeast Asia	1960	100	36.5	27.1	2.5	1.8	4.6	26.2	33.3
	1981	100	18.7	9.9	5.0	4.9	21.3	37.1	63.4
Total	1960	100	43.2	24.7	2.7	2.9	3.6	20.5	26.9
	1981	100	24.3	9.5	6.8	5.4	20.5	31.6	58.8
of which:									
Intra–regional trade	1960	100	44.4	24.7	3.4	2.4	4.4	17.7	25.6
	1981	100	21.8	10.6	8.5	4.8	22.3	30.1	60.9
Inter–regional trade	1960	100	39.7	24.4	0.9	4.8	1.3	28.2	30.4
	1981	100	28.1	7.7	4.0	6.4	17.3	36.0	57.2
All exports	1960	100	48.8	32.3	1.5	7.1	0.9	9.6	12.0
	1981	100	28.5	13.5	4.8	5.8	14.3	30.8	49.9

Source: United Nations Conference on Trade and Development.

Improvements have been realized in the competitive position of many developing countries, particularly the NICs. The prospects are good that trade among developing countries will grow even more in the years ahead because of comparative advantages, increasing incomes and revenues from oil prices.

Developing countries have installed considerable productive capacity and have a growing ability to export manufactured goods, and some technology and services. Four overlapping flows constitute the present trade among developing countries:

1. Manufactured goods—associated with the NICs, these products are concentrated in relatively few countries. Trade among the NIC represents a growing share of their total trade within the LDC ranks.

2. Petroleum—exports of petroleum represent nearly 50 percent of the total value of South-South exports.

3. Primary products—many basic commodities are imported by resource-poor NICs and oil–exporting countries.

4. Neighboring trade—subregional and regional groupings represent a

   growing component of LDC trade, although in most instances they represent less efficient market mechanisms than open trading systems.

A sustained and more diffuse expansion of trade among LDCs require policies and measures to accommodate individual countries. Trade liberalization by other LDCs, particularly in manufacturing, would benefit those countries with appropriate industrial structures and higher levels of income. Special access is important for the exports of the least developed countries (LLDCs) into growing NIC markets, along with efforts on the supply side to assist LLDCs in strengthening their export capacities, including equity investment, technical cooperation, research and training.

Economic Cooperation among Developing Countries (ECDC) is viewed by LDCs as a complement, not a substitute for North-South economic relations. ECDC is thought by the developing countries to improve their bargaining position by some

Table 11.3
Developing Country Trade by Commodity Groups

Exports	Commodity	Total	Fuels	Food	Agricultural raw materials and fertilizers	Chemical products	Steel, iron and nonferrous metals	Machinery and transport equipment	Other manufactures	Total manufactures
From	**To**	$ million				Percentage in 1982				
Intra-Trade										
Americas		21,399	59.5	9.5	2.0	6.2	3.3	8.5	11.0	25.7
Africa		2,440	40.0	25.9	5.5	5.3	3.2	5.0	15.3	25.6
West Asia		15,934	54.5	10.9	1.3	2.2	0.0	11.9	19.3	33.4
S & SE Asia		32,295	31.9	10.2	7.9	5.1	4.8	17.4	22.8	45.2
Developing countries		72,068	45.3	10.7	4.6	4.8	3.2	13.1	18.3	36.1

Inter-Trade

America	Africa	2,771	46.4	29.1	0.9	1.3	2.8	14.8	4.7	20.9
	West Asia	1,927	19.1	47.3	3.4	6.0	7.8	10.2	6.2	22.5
	S & SE Asia	1,956	39.1	16.7	8.1	5.5	16.3	10.2	4.1	19.8
Africa	Americas	4,455	88.8	6.6	2.4	0.2	1.0	0.1	0.9	1.3
	West Asia	1,856	60.2	26.6	1.1	5.0	1.5	0.8	5.0	10.7
	S & SE Asia	1,142	18.5	19.2	10.7	30.6	14.4	0.1	6.6	37.3
West Asia	Americas	9,610	99.6	0.2	0.0	0.1	0.0	0.0	0.0	0.2
	Africa	4,048	75.6	5.3	2.1	1.5	0.0	5.2	10.4	17.0
	S & SE Asia	24,514	97.7	0.3	0.1	1.0	0.0	0.7	0.2	2.0
S & SE Asia	Americas	3,436	27.7	3.8	9.1	2.9	1.5	21.9	33.1	57.9
	Africa	3,930	1.4	19.7	4.5	3.7	1.7	32.5	36.5	72.8
	West Asia	7,909	4.7	20.6	3.3	1.8	6.8	10.7	52.1	64.7
Developing countries	Developing countries	67,554	0.9	0.3	0.1	0.1	0.1	0.2	0.2	0.5

Source: United Nations Council on Trade and Development

what reducing LDC dependence on developed countries. Indeed trade linkages among countries within Asia and Latin America are now sufficiently large to have a bearing on the performance of export sectors and domestic economies in many individual developing countries.

The prospect for increased trade among developing countries is heavily dependent on global economic conditions and could run into some problems because of the declining revenues of oil exporting LDCs, disparity of interest and level of development among the ranks of the many developing countries, and fears of the least developed that dependence on the NICs would in the long run be no better than the relations they presently have with many developed countries. (See Table 11.3.) But the industrialized countries should look favorably on this growing trend of trade between developing countries because it could serve as a means to check their own growing protectionist impulses. New markets for LDC exports, outside of the industrialized world in Europe and North America, would also permit developing countries to sustain their positive rates of economic expansion and earn more exchange, thus increasing income and employment.

Select Bibliography

Agrawala, P.N. *The NIED: An Overview*. New York: Pergamon, 1984.

Beardshaw, Virginia. *Prescription for Change*. London: HAI, 1982.

Frey-Wouters, Ellen. *The European Community and the Third World*. New York: Praeger, 1980.

Friedan, Lennart. *Instability in the International Steel Market*. Stockholm: Beckmans, 1972.

Hansen, Roger. *Beyond the North-South Stalemate*. New York: McGraw-Hill, 1979.

Haq, Khadija. *Equality of Opportunity Within and Among Nations*. New York: Praeger, 1977.

Heller, T. *Poor Health, Rich Profits*. Nottingham, England: Spokesman Books, 1977.

Helms, Robert B., ed. *The International Supply of Medicine*. Washington, D.C.: American Enterprise Institute, 1980.

Jacobson, Henry. *The Emerging International Economic Order*. Santa Barbara, CA: Sage, 1982.

Lodge, Juliet, ed. *Institutions and Policies of the EC*. New York: St. Martin's, 1983.

Melrose, Diana. *The Great Health Robbery*. Oxford: Oxfam, 1981.

Moss, Joanna. *The Lome Conventions and Their Implications for the U.S.* Boulder, CO: Westview, 1982.

Noelke, Michael. *Europe and the Third World*. Brussels: EC Commission, 1979.

Rothstein, Robert. *Global Bargaining, UNCTAD and the Quest for a New International Order*. Princeton, N.J.: Princeton University Press, 1979.

Sauvant, Karl P. *The Group of 77*. New York: Oceana, 1981.

Silverman, Milton, et al. *Prescriptions for Death*. Berkeley: University of California Press, 1982.

Stevens, Christopher. *EEC and the Third World*. London: DDI, 1984.

Valeton, Ida. *Bauxite*. Amsterdam: Elsevier, 1972.

Warren, Kenneth. *World Steel*. New York: Crane-Russak, 1975.

Woods, Douglas, and James C. Burrows. *The World Aluminum-Bauxite Market*. New York: Praeger, 1980.

World Steel Dynamics. New York: Paine Webber Mitchell Hutchins.

Wu, Yuan-Li. *Raw Material Supply in a Multipolar World*. New York: Crane-Russak, 1979.

Index

About the Author

THEODORE R. MALLOCH, formerly a senior economist at the U.S. Senate Foreign Relations Committee and the U.S. State Department, recently joined Wharton Econometrics in Washington, D.C., as Vice President for Consulting and Managing Director of their Washington office.

Prior to joining Wharton, Malloch also worked in international capital markets at Salomon Brothers Inc. in New York. An author of many studies, articles and reviews, Dr. Malloch is a respected political economist with a Ph.D. from the University of Toronto and an M.Litt. degree from the University of Aberdeen in Scotland. His undergraduate work was taken at Gordon College in Massachusetts. A consultant to corporations, banks, foreign governments, research institutes and international organizations, Dr. Malloch has also held various academic appointments and received various awards in the United States and abroad.